52 Weeks of Systematic Theology

How to Easily Understand What Christians Believe—With Clear Weekly Lessons and Practical Application

Welcome Aboard, Check Out This Limited-Time Free Bonus!

Ahoy, reader! Welcome to the Ahoy Publications family, and thanks for snagging a copy of this book! Since you've chosen to join us on this journey, we'd like to offer you something special.

Check out the link below for a FREE e-book filled with delightful facts about American History.

But that's not all - you'll also have access to our exclusive email list with even more free e-books and insider knowledge. Well, what are ye waiting for? Click the link below to join and set sail toward exciting adventures in American History.

Access your bonus here

https://ahoypublications.com/

Or, Scan the QR code!

Table of Contents

INTRODUCTION

Use This Book One Week at a Time: How to Learn Doctrine and Live It

Many Christians love Jesus but feel unsure about what the Bible teaches as a whole. They read Scripture often, yet the big picture feels unclear. Stories, verses, and sermons stay scattered. When questions arise, confidence fades. This book exists to meet that need with care, clarity, and faithfulness to Scripture.

Systematic theology may sound academic, but its purpose is simple. It gathers what the Bible teaches about God and His works and presents it in clear order. It helps believers say what they believe, why they believe it, and how those beliefs shape daily life. Scripture calls God's people to this task. Paul told Timothy to watch his life and his teaching closely (1 Timothy 4:16). Jude urged believers to contend for the faith once delivered to the saints (Jude 3). These commands assume that Christians can know their faith clearly and live it faithfully.

This book invites you to do that one week at a time.

Why This Book Follows a Weekly Rhythm

Most believers live full lives. Work, family, church, and daily duties press in from every side. Long study plans often begin with good intent and end with frustration. A steady rhythm works better. Fifty-two weeks allow truth to grow slowly and take root.

Each chapter in this book is meant for one week. You may read it in one sitting or spread it across several days. The pace matters. Slow reading helps truth settle into the heart. Psalm 1 describes the blessed person as one who meditates on God's law day and night. That picture shows steady attention, not haste.

A weekly pattern also guards against shallow faith. Jesus warned about seed that springs up quickly but fades under pressure because it has no root (Mark 4:16–17). Doctrine grows like roots in soil. It takes time. This book asks for consistency, not speed.

Can one week at a time really shape a life? Yes. Faithful habits form strong believers. Small steps, taken often, lead to lasting growth.

What Systematic Theology Is and Why It Matters

Systematic theology listens to the whole Bible and speaks clearly. It asks direct questions and lets Scripture answer them. Who is God? What is He like? What has He done? What does He require from us? These questions rise from the Bible itself.

Scripture models this approach. Jesus summarized the law and the prophets with clear teaching about loving God and loving others (Matthew 22:37–40). Paul summarized the gospel he preached in plain words rooted in history (1 Corinthians 15:1–4). From the earliest days, the church gathered biblical teaching into clear confession so believers could stand firm.

Doctrine matters because belief shapes life. What you believe about God shapes how you pray. What you believe about sin shapes how you repent. What you believe about Christ shapes how you trust Him. Proverbs 4:23 warns that life flows from the heart. What fills the mind guides the feet.

Some fear that doctrine leads to pride or cold faith. Scripture shows the opposite. True teaching leads to humility, love, and obedience. Paul wrote that sound teaching agrees with godliness (1 Timothy 6:3). When teaching feeds pride, it has already left the path of truth.

Scripture Stands at the Center

This book stands under the authority of the Bible. Scripture rules every chapter. Human words serve only to explain what God has already spoken. Isaiah gave the test long ago: "To the teaching and to the testimony" (Isaiah 8:20).

The Bible is God's breathed-out Word (2 Timothy 3:16). It speaks with unity because one God stands behind it. It carries authority because God Himself speaks through it. This book treats Scripture with reverence and care.

You will see many Bible passages quoted and explained. Read them in your own Bible as well. Context matters. God gave His Word through real people, in real places, across real history. Careful reading honors that gift.

Theology does not replace the Bible. It serves the Bible, much like a map serves a traveler. A map does not replace the land. It helps you walk it with care and confidence.

How This Book Is Organized

This book moves from foundation to fulfillment. Early chapters explain why theology matters and how God speaks. Middle chapters focus on God, His creation, and His saving work in Christ. Later chapters address salvation, the church, and future hope.

Each chapter follows a clear pattern:

- A central theme drawn from Scripture

- Key Bible passages explained in plain language

- Clear statements of Christian belief

- Practical application for everyday life

You may read this book alone or with others. Families, small groups, and church classes can use it together. Scripture teaches that believers grow as they teach and encourage one another (Proverbs 27:17).

Who This Book Serves

This book serves new believers who want a clear path through Christian teaching without heavy terms.

It serves long-time believers who want to revisit familiar truths with fresh focus and care.

It serves teachers and leaders who want a steady guide for a full year of instruction.

It serves any Christian who wants faith rooted in truth and lived with purpose.

If you come with a hunger for God's Word, this book will serve you well. Jesus promised that those who hunger and thirst for righteousness will be filled (Matthew 5:6).

How to Use Each Week Well

Set aside a regular time. Consistency matters more than length. Even twenty focused minutes, used often, bears fruit.

Begin with prayer. Ask God for a teachable heart. Psalm 119:18 offers a simple prayer worth repeating: "Open my eyes, that I may see wondrous things out of your law."

Read slowly. Pause when a sentence calls for thought. Read the Bible passages in full, not just the quoted lines.

Apply what you read. Ask one honest question: how should this truth shape my words, choices, or worship this week? Then answer it with action.

Share what you learn. Teaching others often strengthens faith. God told His people to speak of His words at home and along the way (Deuteronomy 6:6-7).

Doctrine and Daily Life Belong Together

Scripture never separates belief from practice. Jesus said that those who love Him keep His commands (John 14:15). Belief leads to obedience. Obedience flows from belief.

This book presses that connection in every chapter. Teaching without application grows cold. Application without truth grows weak. God calls His people to both.

Belief in God's holiness shapes how we fight sin. Belief in God's grace shapes how we repent after failure. Belief in Christ's return shapes how we use time and resources. Truth moves life.

A Word About Unity and Charity

Christians share core truths of the faith. The chapters in this book reflect that shared confession. On secondary matters, faithful believers may differ. This book aims for clarity without hostility.

Ephesians 4 calls believers to speak the truth in love. Firm belief and gentle speech belong together. This book seeks both.

A Final Invitation

This book asks for one year of steady attention. It does not promise ease, but it offers clarity and hope rooted in Scripture. God honors those who seek Him with sincere hearts.

If you walk through these weeks with prayer and care, you will grow in confidence, joy, and obedience. More than anything, you will grow in love for the God who has made Himself known through His Word and through His Son.

"Now to him who is able to establish you in accordance with my gospel, the message I proclaim about Jesus Christ, in keeping with the revelation of the mystery hidden for long ages past, but now revealed and made known through the prophetic writings by the command of the eternal God, so that all the Gentiles might come to the obedience that comes from faith— to the only wise God be glory forever through Jesus Christ! Amen."
(Romans 16:25–27).

PART ONE
Lay Your Foundation

CHAPTER 1
Start With God, Not Yourself
See Why Theology Matters

Most people begin life by thinking about themselves first. This feels natural. We wake up thinking about our needs, our plans, our fears, and our hopes. Even many spiritual questions begin this way. Why do I feel empty? How can I find peace? What does God want for my life?

Scripture takes a different path. The Bible begins with God.

"In the beginning, God created the heavens and the earth"
(Genesis 1:1).

Before people, before problems, before plans, God stands at the center. That starting point shapes everything else. If we begin with ourselves, faith bends inward. If we begin with God, faith stands firm.

This chapter explains why Christian belief must start with God and why theology matters for every believer, not just pastors or scholars.

God Comes First Because God Is First

God does not enter the story halfway through. He stands at the beginning. He exists before all things and depends on nothing. Scripture repeats this truth in many places.

"Before the mountains were brought forth, or ever you had formed the earth and the world, from everlasting to everlasting you are God" (Psalm 90:2).

God is not part of creation. He is its Maker. He does not grow, change, or learn. He does not wait for human approval. All things come from Him and answer to Him.

This truth shapes how theology works. Theology asks, "What does God say about Himself?" It does not ask, "What do people feel about God?" Feelings change. God does not.

When belief begins with God, it gains stability. When belief begins with human desire, it shifts with every season. Scripture warns about this danger. Paul spoke of people who gathered teachers to suit their own passions (2 Timothy 4:3). That pattern still appears today.

Starting with God guards the church from reshaping Him into our image.

Theology Is About God Before It Is About Us

The word "theology" comes from two Greek words: *theos* (God) and *logos* (word or teaching). Theology means teaching about God. It does not begin with advice for life. It begins with truth about who God is.

This order matters.

If we talk about prayer before we talk about God, prayer turns into a technique.

If we talk about obedience before we talk about God, obedience turns into rule keeping.

If we talk about hope before we talk about God, hope turns into wishful thinking.

Scripture always reveals God before it calls people to respond. The Ten Commandments begin this way: "I am the LORD your God, who brought you out of the land of Egypt" (Exodus 20:2). Only after that statement does God give His commands.

Christian belief follows the same pattern. God acts first. People respond.

Why Many Avoid Theology

Many believers avoid theology because they think it feels cold or distant. Others fear it causes division. Some believe it belongs only to trained leaders.

Scripture does not support these ideas.

The Bible calls all believers to grow in knowledge of God. Paul prayed that believers would grow in knowledge and wisdom so they could live in a way that pleased the Lord (Colossians 1:9–10). Peter urged believers to grow in grace and knowledge of Jesus Christ (2 Peter 3:18).

Avoiding theology does not protect faith. It weakens it.

When believers do not learn what Scripture teaches, other voices fill the gap. Culture teaches. Social media teaches. Personal preference teaches. None of these speak with God's authority.

The choice is not between theology and no theology. The choice is between true teaching and confused teaching.

Right Belief Shapes Right Living

What you believe about God shapes how you live, whether you notice it or not.

✝ If you believe God is distant, prayer fades.

✝ If you believe God is harsh, joy disappears.

✝ If you believe God changes, trust weakens.

✝ If you believe God saves by grace, humility grows.

Scripture ties belief and life together. Paul urged believers to present their bodies as living sacrifices and said this flowed from God's mercy (Romans 12:1). Belief came first. Obedience followed.

Jesus taught the same truth. False belief leads to false fruit. Good trees bear good fruit because of what they are (Matthew 7:17).

Theology shapes the roots. Life shows the fruit.

God Reveals Himself, We Do Not Discover Him

One reason theology begins with God is because people cannot reach Him on their own. God must speak first.

Scripture teaches this clearly. "No one has ever seen God; the only God, who is at the Father's side, he has made him known" (John 1:18).

God reveals Himself through His works and through His Word. Creation shows His glory (Psalm 19:1). Scripture explains His ways. Jesus Christ shows God fully.

This means theology listens before it speaks. It receives before it explains.

When people try to shape belief without God's Word, they drift into guesswork. Paul described this problem when he spoke of people who exchanged the truth about God for a lie (Romans 1:25). That exchange happens whenever human thought replaces God's voice.

Christian theology rests on revelation, not imagination.

Scripture Gives the Pattern for Theology

The Bible does not list doctrines in neat order. Instead, it tells a true story across centuries. Theology gathers that teaching and speaks it clearly.

Scripture itself models this work.

In Nehemiah 8, the priests read the law and gave the sense so the people could grasp it. In Acts 2, Peter explained Scripture and applied it to the crowd. In Acts 17, Paul reasoned from the Scriptures to explain who Jesus is.

These examples show that teaching matters. God's people need explanation, not just reading.

This book follows that pattern. It does not add to Scripture. It explains what Scripture already teaches.

God's Glory Is the Goal of Theology

The purpose of theology is not information alone. Its goal is worship.

Paul ended his teaching in Romans with praise: "For from him and through him and to him are all things. To him be glory forever" (Romans 11:36). After explaining God's plan of salvation, Paul responded with worship.

That pattern matters.

If theology does not lead to praise, something has gone wrong. True teaching humbles the heart and lifts the eyes to God.

Worship grows deeper when belief grows clearer. Singing gains weight. Prayer gains depth. Obedience gains purpose.

Theology serves worship by pointing attention where it belongs.

Starting With Yourself Leads to Confusion

Many modern views of faith begin with personal experience. While experience matters, it cannot lead. Scripture judges experience, not the other way around.

If belief begins with feelings, truth shifts daily. If belief begins with preference, faith turns inward.

Scripture warns against this approach. "There is a way that seems right to a man, but its end is the way to death" (Proverbs 14:12).

Beginning with God corrects vision. It reminds believers that truth exists outside the self. God speaks with authority. People listen with humility.

Theology Guards the Church

False teaching harms the church. Scripture speaks plainly about this danger.

Paul warned elders to watch over the flock because false teachers would arise and twist the truth (Acts 20:29–30). He urged believers to avoid teaching that stirred quarrels and distracted from godly living

(1 Timothy 1:3–7).

Clear theology protects believers. It gives tools to test ideas and reject error.

This does not mean believers argue over every detail. It means they hold firm to core truth and speak with care on lesser matters.

A church grounded in sound teaching stands strong during hardship. A church built on emotion alone fades under pressure.

Theology Helps Believers Suffer Well

Life includes pain. Scripture never hides this fact. The question is not whether suffering will come, but how believers face it.

Belief about God shapes response to suffering.

✝ If God is sovereign, suffering is not pointless.

✝ If God is good, suffering is not cruel.

✝ If God is wise, suffering has purpose.

✝ If God is near, suffering is not lonely.

Job learned this lesson through pain. Though he questioned deeply, he confessed that God knew the way he took (Job 23:10). His belief anchored him.

Theology does not remove pain. It gives strength to endure it.

Theology Forms Humility

Learning about God reveals human limits. Scripture says the fear of the Lord is the beginning of wisdom (Proverbs 9:10). That fear includes reverence and humility.

The more believers learn about God's holiness, the more they see their need for grace. Isaiah saw the Lord's glory and cried out over his sin (Isaiah 6:5). Peter saw Jesus' authority and fell at His knees (Luke 5:8).

True teaching lowers pride and raises gratitude.

Theology Builds Confidence, Not Arrogance

Some fear that learning doctrine leads to arrogance. Scripture addresses this concern. Paul warned that knowledge alone can puff up, but love builds up (1 Corinthians 8:1).

The problem is not learning. The problem is learning without love.

When theology remains tied to Scripture and prayer, it produces confidence with humility. Believers grow steady, not loud. They speak truth with care.

Confidence matters. Believers face questions from the world. They face doubt within their own hearts. Clear belief strengthens faith.

Peter urged believers to be ready to give a reason for their hope, with gentleness and respect (1 Peter 3:15). That readiness requires learning.

Theology Helps Read the Bible Better

Many Christians struggle to read Scripture because they miss the big picture. Stories feel disconnected. Commands feel unclear.

Theology provides structure. It shows how Scripture fits together. It explains how promises lead to fulfillment. It shows how law points to grace.

Jesus explained Scripture this way after His resurrection. He showed how Moses, the Prophets, and the Psalms spoke about Him (Luke 24:27). He gave a framework that brought clarity.

As theology grows, Bible reading grows richer.

God Invites His People to Know Him

God does not hide Himself. He invites His people to know Him.

"You shall know the LORD" appears often in Scripture. Jesus said that eternal life includes knowing the only true God and Jesus Christ (John 17:3).

This knowledge is personal, but it is also true. It rests on God's self-revelation, not human guesswork.

Theology serves that purpose. It helps believers know God as He truly is.

This Book Begins With God on Purpose

This chapter sets the tone for the weeks ahead. Every topic in this book flows from who God is.

✝ Before we speak about Scripture, we speak about God who speaks.

✝ Before we speak about salvation, we speak about God who saves.

✝ Before we speak about the church, we speak about God who calls a people.

✞ Before we speak about hope, we speak about God who reigns. Starting anywhere else leads to confusion.

A Call to Begin Well

This book asks you to begin where Scripture begins. Fix your eyes on God. Let His Word shape belief. Let belief shape life.

Take this week to reflect on who God is. Read passages that speak of His greatness. Pray with reverence. Ask God to teach you through His Word.

Faith grows strongest when it rests on truth. Theology matters because God matters.

"From him and through him and to him are all things. To him be glory forever. Amen" (Romans 11:36).

CHAPTER 2
Build a Simple Map of Christian Belief

Most people would not begin a long trip without a map. They may know where they want to go, but without direction, they lose time, take wrong turns, or give up. Christian belief works the same way. Without a clear structure, Scripture can feel scattered, even though it speaks with one voice.

This chapter explains why believers need a simple map of Christian belief and how that map helps Scripture make sense. The goal is not to replace the Bible but to help believers see how its teaching fits together.

Why Believers Need a Map

The Bible is not a single book. It is a collection of sixty-six books written across many centuries. It includes history, poetry, prophecy, letters, and teaching. God speaks through all of it, but not in the same way on every page.

Many Christians read Scripture faithfully yet struggle to connect its parts. They know stories but miss themes. They know verses but miss context. This leads to confusion.

A map helps solve that problem. It shows the main roads and landmarks. It does not list every detail. It gives orientation.

Christian belief needs the same help. Theology provides structure so truth stays connected. Without it, believers often focus on favorite passages while ignoring others. Over time, belief becomes unbalanced.

Scripture itself encourages order. Paul told Titus to teach what fits with sound doctrine (Titus 2:1). That phrase assumes doctrine has shape and coherence.

What a Theological Map Does

A theological map organizes biblical teaching under clear topics. It asks, what does the whole Bible teach about God, Scripture, sin, Christ, salvation, the church, and the future?

This does not force Scripture into human categories. It listens to Scripture and summarizes what it already teaches.

For example, the Bible does not give one chapter titled "Doctrine of God." Yet it speaks about God everywhere. Theology gathers those passages and states what Scripture teaches clearly and faithfully.

A map also shows how doctrines relate. God's character connects to His actions. Salvation connects to Christ's work. The church connects to God's purpose.

Without these connections, belief feels fragmented.

Scripture Uses Summary Teaching

Some fear that summaries weaken Scripture. The Bible shows otherwise.

Moses summarized God's law for Israel before they entered the land (Deuteronomy 6). Jesus summarized the law and prophets with two commands (Matthew 22:37–40). Paul summarized the gospel message he preached (1 Corinthians 15:1–4).

These summaries did not replace Scripture. They clarified it.

Creeds and confessions serve the same role. They gather biblical truth into clear statements for teaching and protection. They stand under Scripture, not above it.

The Risk of No Map

When believers lack a clear structure, several problems arise.

First, personal preference takes control. People focus on topics they enjoy and avoid those that challenge them. Scripture becomes selective.

Second, false teaching gains ground. Without a clear framework, it becomes hard to spot error. Paul warned that believers could be carried about by every wind of teaching (Ephesians 4:14).

Third, confidence weakens. When questions arise, believers feel unsure where to turn. Faith becomes fragile under pressure.

A simple map guards against these dangers.

What This Map Includes

Christian belief has several core areas. While different traditions may arrange them slightly differently, the substance remains shared across historic Christianity.

This book follows a clear and time-tested structure:

1. God
2. God's Word
3. God's Creation and Rule
4. Sin and God's Justice
5. Jesus Christ
6. Salvation
7. The Church
8. Last Things

Each area builds on the one before it. Together, they tell one unified story.

Start With God

All Christian belief begins with God. Scripture does not begin with human need. It begins with God's action.

"In the beginning, God created the heavens and the earth" (Genesis 1:1).

God's nature explains everything else. His holiness explains sin. His mercy explains grace. His wisdom explains His plan.

If belief begins anywhere else, it loses balance.

Learn How God Speaks

Next comes God's Word. Believers cannot know God rightly unless He speaks. Scripture explains who God is and what He has done.

Paul wrote that Scripture is breathed out by God and useful for teaching, correction, and training in righteousness (2 Timothy 3:16).

Belief without Scripture drifts into opinion. Scripture anchors faith in truth.

See God's Work in Creation and History

God did not create and then step away. He rules over His creation with care.

Scripture teaches that God sustains all things and directs history according to His will (Colossians 1:16–17; Ephesians 1:11).

This doctrine helps believers trust God during hardship. It also shapes how they view work, suffering, and responsibility.

Face Sin Honestly

A faithful map includes the truth about sin. Scripture speaks plainly about human rebellion.

"All have sinned and fall short of the glory of God" (Romans 3:23).

Ignoring sin leads to shallow faith. Facing sin prepares the heart for grace.

The Bible explains how sin entered the world, how it affects every person, and how it brings judgment. This teaching sets the stage for the gospel.

Focus on Jesus Christ

Jesus Christ stands at the center of Christian belief. Every doctrine connects to Him.

Scripture teaches that Jesus is fully God and fully man (John 1:1, 14). He lived in perfect obedience. He died for sinners. He rose from the dead. He reigns as Lord.

Without a clear view of Christ, belief collapses. Jesus is not one topic among many. He is the center that holds all teaching together.

Explain Salvation Clearly

Salvation answers the question every sinner faces: how can people be right with God?

Scripture teaches that salvation comes by grace through faith, not by human effort (Ephesians 2:8–9).

This doctrine explains repentance, faith, new birth, justification, growth in holiness, and perseverance. It guards believers from legalism and despair.

Love the Church

God saves people into a community, not isolation. Scripture calls the church the body of Christ (1 Corinthians 12:27).

Belief about the church shapes worship, service, leadership, and mission. It also shapes how believers care for one another.

A map that ignores the church weakens Christian life.

Live With Hope for the Future

Christian belief ends with hope. Scripture promises resurrection, judgment, and new creation.

This future hope shapes present faithfulness. Paul taught that belief in the resurrection strengthens endurance (1 Corinthians 15:58).

A clear map reminds believers that history moves toward God's promised end.

How the Map Helps Bible Reading

With a clear structure, Scripture reading becomes richer.

Stories connect to doctrine. Promises connect to fulfillment. Commands connect to grace.

For example, laws in the Old Testament make sense when seen in light of God's holiness. Sacrifices point to Christ's work. Psalms express trust rooted in God's character.

The map does not replace careful reading. It supports it.

How the Map Helps Daily Life

Belief shapes choices. A clear map helps believers respond wisely to life's questions.

✝ When suffering comes, belief about God's rule brings peace.

✝ When temptation arises, belief about sin brings caution.

✝ When guilt weighs heavy, belief about grace brings relief.

✝ When death draws near, belief about resurrection brings hope.

Doctrine is not distant. It guides daily faith.

Keeping the Map Simple

A map must stay simple to remain useful. Overloaded detail leads to confusion.

This book focuses on core Christian belief shared across historic Christianity. It explains each topic with clarity and care, avoiding needless debate.

Some topics allow faithful disagreement. This book acknowledges those differences without losing focus on shared truth.

The goal is clarity, not controversy.

Guarding Against Misuse

A map can be misused if treated as final authority. Scripture alone holds that place.

Believers must always test teaching against God's Word (Acts 17:11). Theology serves Scripture, not the other way around.

When the map and the Bible seem to differ, Scripture always corrects the map.

Learning One Section at a Time

This book spreads the map across fifty-two weeks. Each chapter focuses on one part, then connects it to the whole.

You do not need to memorize terms. You need to grasp truth.

Over time, the structure will become familiar. Belief will feel steadier. Scripture will feel clearer.

A Call to Build Carefully

Take this week to reflect on the shape of your belief. Ask yourself honest questions.

✝ Do you see how Scripture fits together?

✝ Do you know why you believe what you believe?

✝ Can you explain the core of your faith with clarity?

These questions are not meant to cause fear. They invite growth.

God calls His people to love Him with heart, soul, and mind (Matthew 22:37). Building a clear map of belief honors that call.

Looking Ahead

The chapters ahead will fill in this map step by step. Each week adds clarity. Each topic connects to the rest.

Begin with patience. Growth takes time. Trust that God uses faithful study to strengthen faith.

"Teach me your way, O LORD, that I may walk in your truth" (Psalm 86:11).

CHAPTER 3
Keep the Gospel at the Center of Everything

Many Christians know the word *gospel*. They hear it preached, sung, and prayed. Yet over time, the gospel can slip from the center of faith and move to the edges. It becomes the message that started the Christian life, not the message that shapes every part of it.

Scripture does not treat the gospel that way. The gospel stands at the center of God's work, God's Word, and the Christian life. When the gospel moves to the center, belief stays clear and life stays grounded. When it drifts to the margins, faith becomes confused, heavy, or shallow.

This chapter explains what the gospel is, why it must remain central, and how it shapes every doctrine and every day.

What the Gospel Is

The gospel is good news, not advice. It tells what God has done, not what people must do to earn His favor.

Paul gave a clear summary of the gospel in Scripture:

"That Christ died for our sins in accordance with the Scriptures, that he was buried, that he was raised on the third day in accordance with the Scriptures" (1 Corinthians 15:3–4).

This message stands at the heart of Christianity. Jesus lived in perfect obedience. He died for sinners. He rose from the dead. He reigns as Lord. All of this happened according to God's plan, revealed in Scripture.

The gospel announces rescue, not self-improvement. It proclaims forgiveness, not moral achievement. It declares peace with God through Christ alone.

Any message that shifts the focus away from Christ's finished work weakens the gospel.

The Gospel Begins With God's Holiness

Good news only makes sense when bad news is clear. Scripture begins the story of salvation with God's holiness.

God is pure, righteous, and set apart from sin. "Holy, holy, holy is the LORD of hosts" (Isaiah 6:3). His holiness reveals the problem humanity faces.

Because God is holy, sin matters. Because God is righteous, justice must be done.

Without this truth, the gospel becomes small. If sin is minor, grace feels unnecessary. If God's holiness is ignored, the cross loses meaning.

The gospel begins with who God is before it speaks of what He gives.

The Gospel Exposes Human Need

Scripture speaks plainly about human sin. "All have sinned and fall short of the glory of God" (Romans 3:23).

Sin is not only wrong action. It is rebellion of the heart. It includes desires, thoughts, and motives that reject God's rule.

The gospel does not flatter people. It tells the truth. Humanity cannot fix itself. No amount of effort can erase guilt or restore fellowship with God.

This truth prepares the way for grace. Until people see their need, they will not value the gift.

The Gospel Centers on Jesus Christ

The gospel is not a set of ideas. It is the announcement of a person and His work.

Jesus Christ stands at the center. He is fully God and fully man. He lived the life sinners could not live. He died the death sinners deserved. He rose in victory over sin and death.

Scripture declares, "There is one mediator between God and men, the man Christ Jesus" (1 Timothy 2:5).

No substitute exists. No addition is needed. Christ's work is complete.

Any teaching that adds human effort as a requirement for acceptance with God shifts the gospel away from its center.

The Gospel Declares Justification by Faith

One of the clearest gospel truths in Scripture is justification by faith alone.

Paul wrote,

> *"We hold that one is justified by faith apart from works of the law" (Romans 3:28).*

Justification means God declares a sinner righteous because of Christ. This declaration rests on Christ's obedience, not human performance.

Faith receives the gift. It does not earn it.

This truth guards believers from pride and despair. Pride fades because salvation rests on grace. Despair fades because salvation does not rest on human strength.

The Gospel Shapes Every Doctrine

The gospel does not belong in one chapter of theology. It connects to every doctrine.

- God's attributes explain why salvation was needed.

- Scripture reveals the promise of salvation.

- Creation shows why sin matters.

- Christology explains how salvation was achieved.

- Salvation doctrine explains how the gift is received.

- The church exists to proclaim the gospel.

- Future hope flows from Christ's resurrection.

When any doctrine drifts away from the gospel, imbalance follows.

For example, teaching about obedience without grace leads to fear. Teaching about grace without obedience leads to carelessness. The gospel holds both together.

The Gospel Guards Against Legalism

Legalism adds rules to grace. It teaches that God's approval must be earned or maintained by performance.

Scripture rejects this idea. Paul warned the Galatians strongly because they added human effort to faith (Galatians 1:6–9).

Legalism shifts focus from Christ to self. It replaces trust with pressure.

The gospel frees believers from this burden. Obedience flows from gratitude, not fear. Good works follow salvation; they do not create it.

The Gospel Guards Against License

Some misunderstand grace and believe obedience no longer matters. Scripture corrects this error as well.

Paul asked, "Shall we continue in sin that grace may abound?" His answer was clear: "By no means" (Romans 6:1-2).

The gospel frees believers from sin's penalty and power. It does not excuse sin.

True faith produces change. Love for Christ leads to obedience.

The gospel keeps grace and holiness together.

The Gospel Shapes Christian Identity

Believers often struggle with identity. They define themselves by success, failure, past sin, or present struggle.

The gospel speaks a better word.

In Christ, believers are forgiven, adopted, and made new. Paul wrote that if anyone is in Christ, he is a new creation (2 Corinthians 5:17).

This identity rests on God's declaration, not human feeling. Even on hard days, the gospel remains true.

Living from gospel identity brings peace and stability.

The Gospel Shapes Worship

Worship flows from gratitude. When the gospel stays central, worship stays sincere.

Songs gain meaning. Prayer gains depth. Scripture reading gains joy.

Paul urged believers to present themselves to God because of His mercy (Romans 12:1). Mercy came first. Worship followed.

When worship loses the gospel, it becomes routine or performance. When the gospel remains central, worship becomes response.

The Gospel Shapes Prayer

Prayer often drifts into habit or duty. The gospel restores confidence.

Because of Christ, believers approach God as children, not strangers. Hebrews teaches that believers may draw near with confidence because of Jesus' work (Hebrews 4:16).

Prayer rests on grace, not worthiness.

This truth invites honesty, repentance, and trust.

The Gospel Shapes Suffering

Suffering tests faith. Pain raises hard questions. The gospel does not remove suffering, but it gives meaning and hope.

Christ suffered first. He entered human pain and overcame it through resurrection.

Scripture teaches that present suffering does not compare with future glory (Romans 8:18).

The gospel assures believers that suffering is not punishment for sin. Christ bore that punishment fully.

This truth anchors faith during hardship.

The Gospel Shapes Community

The church exists because of the gospel. People from different backgrounds become one body through Christ.

Paul reminded believers that they were united by grace, not status or effort (Ephesians 2:8-16).

When the gospel stays central, pride fades and patience grows. Forgiveness flows more freely. Unity strengthens.

When the gospel fades, division grows.

The Gospel Shapes Mission

The church's mission flows directly from the gospel.

Jesus commanded His followers to make disciples and teach all He commanded (Matthew 28:18-20). That command rests on His authority and saving work.

Mission is not about building institutions or gaining influence. It is about announcing good news.

When the gospel stays central, mission stays clear.

The Gospel Shapes Daily Obedience

Christian obedience is often misunderstood. Some see it as payment to God. Others see it as optional.

Scripture teaches a different view. Obedience is a response of love.

Jesus said that those who love Him keep His commands (John 14:15). Love grows from grace.

The gospel motivates obedience through gratitude and trust.

Keeping the Gospel Central Takes Care

Drift happens slowly. Over time, believers may assume the gospel and focus on other things.

Paul warned the Corinthians to hold fast to the gospel they received (1 Corinthians 15:1–2). That warning remains needed.

Keeping the gospel central requires regular return to Scripture. It requires preaching, teaching, and reminding.

Believers never outgrow the gospel. They grow deeper into it.

Signs the Gospel Has Drifted

Several signs reveal when the gospel has moved off center.

- Faith feels heavy rather than joyful
- Obedience feels forced rather than willing
- Failure leads to despair rather than repentance
- Pride grows in success
- Fear grows in weakness

Returning to the gospel restores balance.

A Simple Way to Keep the Gospel Central

One helpful practice is to ask simple questions often.

- What has God done for me in Christ?
- What does this passage reveal about grace?
- How does Christ's work shape my response today?

These questions keep focus where it belongs.

The Gospel and the Whole Christian Life

The gospel does not end at conversion. It shapes the whole Christian life from beginning to end.

Paul wrote that he lived by faith in the Son of God who loved him and gave Himself for him (Galatians 2:20). That statement describes daily life, not only the past.

Believers grow by returning to the same good news again and again.

A Call to Keep the Center Clear

Take this week to reflect on the place of the gospel in your faith.

✝ Do you return to Christ's work often?

✝ Do you rest in grace when you fail?

✝ Do you obey from gratitude rather than fear?

These questions invite honesty, not guilt.

God's grace remains steady. Christ's work remains complete. The gospel remains good news.

Keep it at the center.

"For I am not ashamed of the gospel, for it is the power of God for salvation to everyone who believes" (Romans 1:16).

CHAPTER 4
Learn From Creeds and Confessions Without Replacing Scripture

Many Christians feel unsure about creeds and confessions. Some see them as old documents with little use today. Others worry they might replace the Bible or limit personal faith. Still others have never read one and do not know why churches use them at all.

Scripture gives a better path. Creeds and confessions can serve the church well when they stay in their proper place. They do not replace Scripture. They serve it. They do not rule faith. They guard it.

This chapter explains what creeds and confessions are, why the church has used them, and how believers can benefit from them without giving them authority that belongs to Scripture alone.

What Creeds and Confessions Are

A creed is a brief statement of belief. The word comes from the Latin *credo*, meaning "I believe." Creeds summarize core Christian truth in clear and careful language.

A confession is longer and more detailed. It explains belief across many topics, such as God, Scripture, salvation, and the church.

Both aim to say clearly what the Bible teaches.

For example, the Apostles' Creed gives a short summary of Christian belief about God the Father, Jesus Christ, the Holy Spirit, the church, forgiveness, resurrection, and eternal life. Confessions, such as the Westminster Confession or the Augsburg Confession, explain these beliefs in greater detail.

Neither adds new teaching. Both aim to state biblical teaching clearly.

Why the Early Church Used Creeds

Creeds did not appear because believers wanted to complicate faith. They appeared because the church faced serious challenges.

From the beginning, false teaching threatened the church. Some denied that Jesus was truly human. Others denied that He was truly God. Some rejected the Trinity. Others changed the gospel.

The church responded by stating clearly what Scripture teaches.

Paul warned Timothy to guard the good deposit entrusted to him (2 Timothy 1:14). Jude urged believers to contend for the faith once delivered to the saints (Jude 3). These commands required clarity.

Creeds helped the church confess truth together and reject error together.

Scripture Models Confession of Faith

The Bible itself contains short confessions.

Israel confessed, "Hear, O Israel: The LORD our God, the LORD is one" (Deuteronomy 6:4). That statement shaped worship and identity.

Peter confessed, "You are the Christ, the Son of the living God" (Matthew 16:16). Jesus affirmed that confession.

Paul wrote that believers confess that Jesus is Lord (Romans 10:9). That confession carried meaning and cost.

These statements show that clear confession belongs to biblical faith.

Creeds Do Not Replace Scripture

Scripture alone holds final authority. Creeds and confessions serve Scripture, not the other way around.

The Bible teaches this plainly. Scripture is God-breathed and sufficient for teaching and correction (2 Timothy 3:16–17). No human document carries that authority.

Faithful churches treat creeds as helpful guides, not binding rulers. They use them to explain Scripture, not to silence Scripture.

When creeds stay under the Bible, they serve well. When they rise above it, they cause harm.

Why Creeds Still Matter Today

Some argue that modern believers do not need creeds because they have the Bible. That argument misunderstands how creeds work.

Creeds do not replace Bible reading. They help believers read the Bible more clearly.

Every believer already has beliefs about God, Christ, and salvation. The question is whether those beliefs match Scripture.

Creeds make belief visible. They help believers say clearly what they believe and test it against God's Word.

Without clear statements, belief becomes vague. Vague belief weakens faith.

Creeds Protect the Gospel

Throughout history, creeds have guarded the church during seasons of confusion.

The Nicene Creed, for example, defended the truth that Jesus is fully God. Without that truth, the gospel collapses. Only God can save. Only God can forgive sin fully.

By stating biblical truth clearly, creeds helped the church remain faithful to Scripture.

They still serve that purpose today.

Creeds Teach the Faith Clearly

Creeds help teach both new and mature believers.

New believers often ask basic questions. Who is God? Who is Jesus? What does the church believe? Creeds offer clear answers rooted in Scripture.

Mature believers benefit as well. Repeating core truth shapes memory and guards belief over time.

Scripture calls God's people to teach truth carefully. Paul urged Titus to teach what fits with sound doctrine (Titus 2:1). Creeds help do that work.

Creeds Help the Church Speak Together

Christian faith is not private opinion. It is shared confession.

When believers confess the same truth together, unity grows. Worship gains depth. Teaching gains clarity.

The early church devoted itself to the apostles' teaching (Acts 2:42). That teaching formed a shared belief.

Creeds help churches speak with one voice about core truth.

Creeds Do Not End Disagreement

Creeds do not solve every debate. Faithful believers may still differ on secondary matters.

That is not a failure. Scripture itself shows room for growth and discussion.

Creeds focus on core truth. They draw clear lines where Scripture speaks clearly. They allow room where Scripture allows room.

This balance matters.

Confessions Provide Greater Detail

While creeds summarize belief, confessions explain it more fully.

Confessions often address topics such as Scripture, God's attributes, salvation, the church, and future hope. They explain how these truths connect.

Confessions help churches teach carefully and consistently.

They also help leaders guard teaching within the church.

Confessions and Church Accountability

Confessions often serve as teaching standards for pastors and elders. This protects congregations from sudden shifts in belief.

Paul urged church leaders to hold firm to the trustworthy word as taught (Titus 1:9). Confessions help leaders do that work with care.

This does not remove the need for Bible study. It strengthens it.

Reading Creeds Wisely

Creeds should be read slowly and carefully. They deserve attention, not blind acceptance.

Believers should ask honest questions:

✝ What Scripture supports this statement?

✝ How does this line protect the gospel?

✝ Does this confession reflect the Bible's teaching clearly?

The Bereans tested teaching against Scripture (Acts 17:11). That example still guides believers today.

Common Fears About Creeds

Some fear that creeds limit personal faith. Scripture answers that fear.

True freedom comes from truth, not confusion. Jesus said that truth sets people free (John 8:32).

Creeds do not limit Scripture. They limit error.

Others fear creeds create pride. That danger exists if creeds are used harshly. Scripture warns against pride in all areas of faith.

When creeds are used humbly, they build faith rather than inflate ego.

Creeds and Church History

Creeds connect believers to the wider church across time.

Christian faith did not begin last century. Believers today stand in a long line of faithful witnesses.

Hebrews 12 speaks of a great cloud of witnesses. Creeds echo that shared testimony.

Reading creeds reminds believers that the faith has endured trials, questions, and opposition before.

Creeds and Personal Faith

Creeds are not meant only for public worship. They also shape personal faith.

Reciting core truth strengthens memory. It steadies belief during doubt. It reminds believers of truth during prayer.

Many believers have found comfort in confessing truth during hardship.

Truth spoken often sinks deep.

Scripture Remains the Final Word

This truth must remain clear. Scripture alone rules faith.

If a creed ever conflicts with Scripture, Scripture corrects the creed.

The church has revised and refined confessions across history because Scripture stands above them.

That humility honors God.

This Book and Creeds

This book draws from historic Christian teaching shared across centuries. It reflects truth confessed by the church through time.

It does not require agreement with every historic document. It focuses on shared core belief grounded in Scripture.

Creeds inform this book. Scripture governs it.

Learning From Creeds Without Fear

Believers need not fear creeds. Used rightly, they serve as helpful tools.

✝ They summarize truth.

✝ They guard the gospel.

✝ They teach clearly.

✝ They connect believers across time.

They do all this while standing under Scripture.

A Call to Learn With Discernment

Take this week to reflect on the place of shared confession in your faith.

✝ Do you know the core truths Christians have confessed across history?

✝ Can you state what you believe with clarity?

✝ Do you test all teaching by God's Word?

These questions encourage growth, not pressure.

God has preserved His truth through faithful teaching across generations. Creeds stand as witnesses to that care.

Hold fast to Scripture. Learn from the church. Confess truth with humility.

"Stand firm and hold to the traditions that you were taught by us" (2 Thessalonians 2:15).

PART TWO
Trust God's Word

CHAPTER 5
Receive God's Revelation as a Gift

Most people want to know the truth about life. They look at the stars and wonder where the world came from. They look at their own hearts and wonder why they feel both wonder and guilt. People try to find God through logic, meditation, or nature. But there is a problem. A person can no more discover God on their own than an ant can understand the mind of a mathematician. If we want to know God, He must speak first.

This chapter looks at how God makes Himself known. This process is called revelation. It is a gift because God does not owe us an explanation of Himself. He chooses to pull back the curtain. He shows us His power, His character, and His plan. Without this gift, we would be left to guess. Guessing about God leads to fear or confusion. Receiving His revelation leads to peace and certainty.

God Speaks Through What He Made

The first way God reveals Himself is through the world around us. This is often called general revelation. It is general because it goes out to all people in all places at all times. No one is missed by this message. The sun rises on every continent. The mountains stand tall for every culture to see.

Scripture says that the heavens declare the glory of God (Psalm 19:1). When you look at a sunset, you see His beauty. When you look at the vastness of the ocean, you see His power. The complexity of a single human cell shows His wisdom. Nature acts like a giant mirror. It reflects the qualities of the Person who made it.

The Message Is Clear to Everyone

This message is loud and clear. Romans 1 says that God's invisible attributes are clearly perceived in the things that have been made. This means no one can say they did not know a Creator exists. Even people who have never read a Bible can see that the world has a Designer.

General revelation tells us three main things. First, God is powerful. Only an almighty Being could create the universe from nothing. Second, God is wise. The balance of the planets and the seasons shows a brilliant mind. Third, God is good. He provided food, water, and beauty for us to enjoy.

The Limits of General Revelation

But general revelation has limits. It tells us that God is there, but it does not tell us how to be saved. It shows us His power, but it does not tell us His name. Nature shows us that we are small and that God is great. It often leaves us with a sense of guilt because we know we have not honored the Creator. For a solution to that guilt, we need a second gift.

God Speaks Through His Word

While nature gives us a general picture, Scripture gives us a specific one. This is called special revelation. God moved beyond the stars and spoke in human language. He used words we can understand. He spoke to prophets and apostles. Eventually, these words were written down in the Bible.

Special revelation is necessary because sin clouded our vision. While the world is still beautiful, it is also broken. We see storms, disease, and death. If we only looked at nature, we might wonder if God is angry or indifferent. Special revelation clears up the confusion. It tells us the story of why the world is broken and how God is fixing it.

God Reveals His Character and Name

In the Bible, God reveals His specific character. We learn that He is holy, meaning He is set apart from sin. We learn that He is merciful, meaning He treats us better than we deserve.

Most importantly, we learn about His covenants. A covenant is a formal agreement or promise. Through these promises, God binds Himself to His people. He tells us His name, Yahweh. He tells us His laws. He tells us His plan to rescue humanity.

The Ultimate Revelation: Jesus Christ

The highest point of God's revelation is not a book or a mountain. It is a Person. Hebrews 1 says that in many times and many ways, God spoke to our fathers by the prophets. But in these last days, He has spoken to us by His Son. Jesus Christ is the Word made flesh.

If you want to know what God is like, look at Jesus. When Jesus healed the sick, He showed God's compassion. When Jesus calmed the storm,

He showed God's authority. When Jesus died on the cross, He showed God's love and justice meeting together. Jesus did not just talk about God; He revealed God perfectly.

Jesus Is the Clear Face of God

Jesus said, "Whoever has seen me has seen the Father" (John 14:9). This is the center of our faith. We do not follow a set of abstract ideas. We follow a living Lord who walked on this earth. He is the clearest "word" God has ever spoken. Through Jesus, we see that God is not just a distant Creator. He is a Father who seeks the lost.

Why Revelation Matters for Your Daily Life

You might think that the concept of revelation is only for scholars. But it changes how you live every day. First, it gives you a firm place to stand. In a world where everyone has a different opinion, you have a message from God. You do not have to wonder what is right or wrong. You do not have to invent your own purpose for living. God has told you why you are here.

Revelation Produces True Humility

Second, revelation produces humility. We did not find God through our own brilliance. We did not solve the mystery of the universe. God reached down to us. This keeps us from being arrogant about our faith. We are simply people who have received a gift. Our job is to listen and obey, not to edit what God has said.

See the World With New Eyes

Third, it changes how you see the world. When you walk through a park, you are not just looking at trees. You are looking at God's artwork. When you read your Bible, you are not just reading history. You are hearing the Creator of the universe speak to you. This makes life more vibrant and meaningful.

Trusting the Gift

Receiving a gift requires trust. If a friend gives you a map, you have to trust that the map is accurate before you follow it. God has given us the map of His revelation. We must decide if we will trust it.

Some people want more revelation. They want God to write their name in the clouds or speak in an audible voice. But God has already given us what we need. He gave us the glory of creation. He gave us the depth of the Scriptures. He gave us the life of His Son. If we ignore what He has already said, we will not listen to more.

Faith Begins With Gratitude

Faith begins by saying "thank you" for the gift of revelation. It means opening the Bible with the expectation that God is speaking. It means looking at the world with eyes of worship. It means looking to Jesus as the final answer to every big question.

God's Revelation Is Sufficient

We do not need to look for secret messages or hidden signs. God is not trying to hide from us. He has spoken clearly. His Word provides everything we need for life and godliness. When we study theology, we are simply organizing what God has already revealed. We are not discovering new truths; we are learning to love the truth He already gave us.

Respond to the Light

Revelation is like a light in a dark room. Once the light is on, you can see where to walk. You can see the obstacles and the path. God has turned the light on through His Word and His Son. The only question is whether we will walk in that light or close our eyes.

Weekly Belief Statement

We believe that God has graciously made Himself known to all people through the things He has created. We also believe He has spoken specifically through the Holy Scriptures and perfectly through His Son, Jesus Christ. This revelation is true, sufficient, and necessary for us to know God and live for His glory.

Practical Application

- **Look Up:** Spend ten minutes this week outside without your phone. Look at the sky, the plants, or the animals. Identify three things that show God's power or wisdom. Use those things as prompts for a short prayer of praise.

- **Listen In:** When you read your Bible this week, stop asking "What does this mean to me?" and first ask "What does this tell me about God?" List the attributes of God you find in the passage.

- **Focus on Christ:** Read the first chapter of the Gospel of John. Pay attention to how Jesus is called "the Word." Reflect on how Jesus makes the Father known in ways that nature cannot.

- **Share the Gift:** Think of a friend who is confused about the meaning of life. Instead of giving them your opinion, share one thing God has revealed about Himself in His Word.

Audit Your Influences: Look at the voices you listen to most during the week. Do they align with what God has revealed? If they contradict God's Word, consider limiting those influences to keep your mind clear.

"The secret things belong to the Lord our God, but the things that are revealed belong to us and to our children forever, that we may do all the words of this law." - Deuteronomy 29:29.

CHAPTER 6
Trust the Bible as God's Written Word

Most people have a book that changed their life. It might be a story that sparked their imagination or a guide that taught them a new skill. But the Bible is different from every other book ever written. It does not just contain good advice or interesting history. It is the very Word of God.

This claim is bold. If the Bible is just a human book, we can take what we like and leave the rest. But if it is God's written Word, it has the right to command our lives. This chapter explains why we can trust the Bible. We will look at how God used human authors to write His message and why that message remains perfect today. Trusting the Bible is the foundation for everything else we believe.

The Source of the Message

When we talk about the Bible, we use the word "inspiration." In common language, we say a sunset is inspiring or an athlete is inspired. But in theology, the word has a specific meaning. It comes from a Greek word that means "God-breathed."

The Apostle Paul wrote that all Scripture is breathed out by God (2 Timothy 3:16). This means the words on the pages of your Bible did not start with man. They started with God. Just as you use your breath to form words when you speak, God used His Spirit to produce the written Word.

This does not mean the Bible fell from the sky. God did not bypass the minds of the people who wrote it. He worked through them. This is the beauty of how God communicates. He uses human language and human history to tell His eternal story.

How God Used Human Authors

God chose about forty different men over a span of 1,500 years to write the books of the Bible. These men came from many walks of life. Some were kings, like David and Solomon. Others were simple fishermen, like Peter and John. One was a doctor, and another was a tax collector.

They wrote in different places and during different times. They used different styles, such as poetry, history, and letters. Yet, despite these differences, the Bible tells one unified story. It has one consistent message about God's glory and man's salvation.

How is this possible? The Apostle Peter explains that no prophecy was ever produced by the will of man. Instead, men spoke from God as they were carried along by the Holy Spirit (2 Peter 1:21). Imagine a boat with its sails caught in the wind. The boat moves, but the wind is the power that directs it. In the same way, the Holy Spirit directed the authors to write exactly what God intended, without removing their individual personalities.

The Bible Is Without Error

Because God is the primary author of the Bible, the Bible is true. God is the source of all truth. He cannot lie, and He does not make mistakes. Therefore, His Word cannot contain errors. This is often called "inerrancy."

This means that when the Bible speaks on any subject, it speaks the truth. It is true when it tells us about the beginning of the world. It is true when it records the history of Israel. It is true when it explains the way of salvation. We do not have to pick through the Bible to find which parts are "pure" and which parts are "flawed."

If we start to believe the Bible has errors, we lose our foundation. Who would decide which parts are right and which are wrong? We would become the judges of God's Word instead of the Word being the judge of us. Trusting the Bible means believing that God is capable of preserving His message perfectly.

The Bible Is Our Final Authority

Since the Bible is God's Word, it holds the highest authority in our lives. Authority means the right to rule or give commands. We live under many authorities, like laws, employers, or parents. But the Bible is the ultimate authority because it comes from the King of kings.

In the early church, believers did not rely on their feelings or the opinions of the culture. They went to the Scriptures. When Jesus was tempted in the wilderness, He answered every temptation by saying, "It is written." He did not argue with logic; He stood on the authority of the Word.

If the Bible says something is a sin, it is a sin, regardless of what society says. If the Bible makes a promise, that promise is certain, regardless of how we feel. When we submit to the authority of the Word, we find true freedom. We stop drifting in the sea of human opinion and start building on a rock.

The Bible Is Sufficient for Us

Some people worry that the Bible is an old book that cannot help with modern problems. They look for new revelations or secret knowledge. But the Bible is sufficient. This means it contains everything we need to know God, to be saved, and to live a life that pleases Him.

Scripture says the Word of God is able to make us "complete, equipped for every good work" (2 Timothy 3:17). If you have the Bible, you have enough. You do not need a special vision to know God's will. You do not need a new philosophy to find peace. The Bible provides the answers to our deepest questions about identity, purpose, and the future.

While we can learn helpful things from science, history, or psychology, these things are secondary. The Bible is the primary lens through which we see the world. It gives us the big picture that makes sense of everything else.

The Power of the Written Word

The Bible is not a dead book. It is living and active (Hebrews 4:12). It has the power to change hearts. Have you ever read a verse and felt like it was reading you? That is because the Holy Spirit uses the Word to convict us of sin and comfort us in sorrow.

The words of men can inform us, but only the Word of God can transform us. It works like a mirror, showing us who we really are. It works like a lamp, showing us where to walk. It works like fire, refining our character. When you read the Bible, you are not just gaining information. You are encountering the power of God.

Why We Can Trust the Preservation of the Bible

Some people ask how we can know the Bible we have today is the same as what was originally written. They worry that errors crawled in during the process of copying the text. This is a fair question, and history gives us a confident answer.

Thousands of ancient manuscripts exist today. When scholars compare these manuscripts, they find incredible agreement. The variations that do exist are usually small things, like spelling or word order, which do not change any doctrine. God did not just inspire the writing of the Word; He has been faithful to preserve it through the centuries.

The discovery of the Dead Sea Scrolls in 1947 is a great example. These scrolls were over a thousand years older than the copies we had at the time. When experts compared them, they found that the text had remained almost exactly the same. God has watched over His Word to ensure we have exactly what He wants us to have.

Reading the Bible With Faith

Trusting the Bible as God's Word changes how we read it. We do not read it to find faults. We read it to find God. This requires a heart of faith. We must come to the text with a desire to hear from our Creator.

If we encounter something we do not understand, we do not assume the Bible is wrong. We assume our understanding is limited. We pray for the Holy Spirit to help us. We study with humility. We remember that the God who made the universe is much larger than our minds. Trusting the Bible means trusting God's character.

The Word Stands Forever

Human ideas come and go. Best-selling books today will be forgotten in fifty years. Scientific theories are often replaced by new ones. But the Word of God does not change. Isaiah 40:8 says, "The grass withers, the flower fades, but the word of our God will stand forever."

Because the Bible is eternal, it is always relevant. It spoke to people in ancient Israel, and it speaks to people in the digital age. It addresses the same human needs: the need for hope, the need for forgiveness, and the need for a relationship with God. You can build your life on the Bible because it is the only thing in this world that will never move.

Weekly Belief Statement

We believe the Bible is the Word of God, fully inspired by the Holy Spirit. We believe it is without error in its original writings and carries final authority in all matters of faith and life. We trust that God has preserved His Word for us and that it is sufficient for our salvation and growth in Christ.

Practical Application

✝ **Start With Prayer:** Before you read the Bible this week, say a simple prayer: "Lord, I believe this is Your Word. Please help me see the truth and obey it."

✝ **Memorize a Verse:** Choose a verse about the Word of God, such as Psalm 119:105 or 2 Timothy 3:16. Write it on a card and repeat it to yourself throughout the day.

✝ **Compare the Word:** Think of a common piece of advice you hear in the world today. Look up what the Bible says about that topic. Practice letting the Bible have the final say.

✝ **Thank God for the Authors:** Reflect on the fact that God used real people with real lives to write His Word. Thank Him for the way He meets us in our human experience.

✝ **Build a Habit:** Commitment follows trust. If you truly believe the Bible is God speaking to you, make it a priority to listen every day. Set a specific time this week to read at least one chapter.

"All Scripture is breathed out by God and profitable for teaching, for reproof, for correction, and for training in righteousness" (2 Timothy 3:16).

CHAPTER 7
Read the Bible as True and Reliable

Many people today view the Bible as a collection of myths or moral fables. They might respect its impact on history, but they doubt its facts. They wonder if the stories of the Exodus, the miracles of Elijah, or the resurrection of Jesus actually happened. This doubt creates a shaky foundation for faith. If the history in the Bible is not true, why should we trust its promises?

This chapter focuses on why we can read the Bible as a record of real events. We call this the reliability of Scripture. God did not give us a book of abstract philosophy. He gave us a book rooted in time and space. He worked through real people, in real places, and during real events. When we see the Bible as reliable, our confidence in God grows.

Faith Is Rooted in History

Christianity is a historical faith. It does not depend on secret feelings but on public facts. If you remove the history from the Bible, the theology falls apart. For example, if Jesus did not actually rise from the grave, our faith is useless (1 Corinthians 15:14).

The writers of the Bible were very careful to mention names, dates, and locations. They wanted readers to know these things truly happened. Luke, who wrote a Gospel and the book of Acts, stated that he investigated everything carefully from the beginning. He wanted his readers to have certainty about the things they had been taught (Luke 1:3-4).

When you read the Bible, you are reading the testimony of people who saw God act. They were not making up "cleverly devised myths" (2 Peter 1:16). They were witnesses. They saw the blind receive sight. They saw the Red Sea part. They recorded these things so that we could believe.

Archaeology Supports the Record

Over the last two centuries, archaeology has provided a wealth of evidence for the Bible's reliability. Time after time, discoveries have confirmed the biblical record. In the past, critics doubted that certain kings or nations mentioned in the Bible ever existed. But as shovels hit the dirt, the evidence appeared.

For instance, critics once claimed the Hittite Empire was a biblical myth. Then, archaeologists discovered the Hittite capital in modern-day Turkey. Others doubted that King David was a real historical figure. Then, the Tel Dan Stele was found, an ancient stone mention of the "House of David."

Archaeology does not "prove" every spiritual truth in the Bible, but it does show that the Bible is accurate when it describes the world. It places the stories of Scripture in the real world of the ancient Near East. This gives us confidence that the authors were writing about things they knew firsthand.

The Bible Explains the World as It Is

One way to test if a book is reliable is to see if it matches reality. The Bible offers a view of the world that makes sense of our experience. It describes the beauty of creation and the depth of human corruption. It explains why we crave justice and why we struggle with guilt.

If the Bible were a book of human inventions, it would likely be more one-sided. It would make its heroes look perfect. Instead, it shows the flaws of its greatest figures. It records Peter's denial, David's adultery, and Moses' anger. This honesty is a mark of reliability. The Bible tells the truth, even when the truth is uncomfortable.

When we read the Bible, we see a mirror of our own lives. We see that the problems people faced thousands of years ago, fear, pride, and the need for hope, are the same problems we face today. A book that understands the human heart so well is a book we can trust.

The Internal Consistency of the Word

The Bible is made of sixty-six books written by many authors. Yet, it displays a remarkable unity. From Genesis to Revelation, it follows a single plot: God's creation, man's fall, God's redemption through Christ, and the future restoration of all things.

If you asked five people today to write their opinions on God, you would get five different answers. The Bible has forty authors over fifteen centuries, yet they do not contradict each other on the core message. This internal consistency is a powerful argument for its reliability. It shows that one Mind was directing the entire process.

The Old Testament contains hundreds of prophecies about the coming Messiah. These were written centuries before Jesus was born. Jesus fulfilled these prophecies in detail, from His birthplace in Bethlehem to the way He died. The odds of this happening by chance are impossible. This level of accuracy proves that the Bible is a reliable guide to God's plan.

Trusting the New Testament Documents

Some people worry that the stories of Jesus were changed over time, like a game of "telephone." But the New Testament was written very close to the events it describes. Most of the books were written within thirty to sixty years of Jesus' death. This is extremely fast for ancient history.

Because the books were written so early, many people who had seen Jesus were still alive. If the apostles had lied about the miracles or the resurrection, people would have corrected them. Instead, the message spread rapidly because people knew it was true.

Furthermore, the early Christians were willing to die for this message. People might die for something they think is true, but they do not die for something they know is a lie. The courage of the early church is a testament to the reliability of what they had seen and heard.

Reliability Leads to Responsibility

If the Bible is reliable, we cannot ignore it. If the events it records are true, then the God it describes is real. This means we have a responsibility to respond to what He has said.

Reading the Bible as reliable changes our attitude. We no longer ask, "Is this true?" Instead, we ask, "What does this mean for my life?" We stop treating the Bible as a cafeteria where we pick and choose. We treat it as a map that we must follow if we want to reach our destination.

When you trust that the Bible is reliable, you find a sense of peace. You don't have to worry that a new discovery will suddenly prove your faith wrong. You can rest in the fact that God's Word has stood the test of time and the scrutiny of critics. It remains the most reliable book in the world.

Faith and Facts Work Together

Some think that faith means "believing something you know isn't true." But biblical faith is different. Biblical faith is "trusting in what you have good reason to believe is true." God gives us enough evidence to see that His Word is reliable, and then He calls us to trust Him.

The facts of the Bible provide the ground for our faith to grow. We don't have to check our brains at the door when we enter a church. We can bring our questions and our doubts to the Word. Time and again, the Bible proves itself to be a sturdy anchor for the soul.

Weekly Belief Statement

We believe that the Bible is a reliable and accurate record of God's work in history. We believe that the events described in Scripture truly occurred and that the testimony of the authors is trustworthy. We reject the idea that the Bible is a collection of myths, and we hold that its historical truth provides a firm foundation for our faith and life.

Practical Application

- **Verify a Fact:** Choose a historical person or place in the Bible, such as Pontius Pilate or the city of Ephesus. Do a quick search to see what history and archaeology say about them. Notice how the Bible matches the historical record.

- **Read an Eye-Witness Account:** Read the first chapter of 1 John. Notice how the author emphasizes what he has seen, heard, and touched. Reflect on why this "witness" language matters for your trust in the Bible.

- **Address a Doubt:** If there is a story in the Bible you find hard to believe, don't ignore it. Write it down and look for resources that explain the historical and biblical context of that event.

- **Thank God for Truth:** In your prayers this week, thank God that He did not leave us with guesses, but gave us a record of His real acts in the real world.

- **Look for Consistency:** As you read your Bible this week, try to find a connection between the Old Testament and the New Testament. Look at how a promise in the past is kept in the future.

"For we did not follow cleverly devised myths when we made known to you the power and coming of our Lord Jesus Christ, but we were eyewitnesses of his majesty"
(2 Peter 1:16).

CHAPTER 8
Interpret Scripture With Care and Humility

Imagine receiving a letter from a loved one. To understand it, you need to know who wrote it, why they wrote it, and what the words meant to them. If you pull one sentence out of the middle without looking at the rest, you might get the wrong idea. The same is true for the Bible. Because the Bible is a big book written a long time ago, we must learn how to read it correctly.

This chapter focuses on interpretation. This is the process of discovering what God actually said so we do not make the Bible say what we want it to say. Proper interpretation requires both a good method and a humble heart. When we interpret Scripture with care, we protect ourselves from error and hear God's voice more clearly.

Seek the Author's Original Meaning

The first rule of reading the Bible is to ask: "What did the author mean when he first wrote this to his original audience?" Every book of the Bible was written by a real person to a specific group of people for a specific reason.

If we ignore the original setting, we will likely misinterpret the text. For example, when we read a letter Paul wrote to the church in Corinth, we should try to understand the problems that church was facing. We aren't just reading "to us"; we are reading "through them."

To find the original meaning, we look at the context. Context is everything around a verse. This includes the verses right before and after it, the purpose of the whole book, and the historical setting of the time. A text without a context is just a pretext for making it say whatever you want.

Let Scripture Explain Scripture

One of the most helpful principles of interpretation is that the Bible is its own best teacher. Because the Holy Spirit is the ultimate author of the entire Bible, one part of Scripture will never contradict another part.

If you find a passage that seems difficult or confusing, look for other passages that are clearer on the same topic. This is often called the "analogy of faith." We use the clear parts of the Bible to help us understand the harder parts.

For instance, if you read a verse that seems to suggest we earn our way to heaven, you should look at the many clear verses that state salvation is a gift of grace through faith. We do not build a whole belief system on one obscure verse. We look at the weight of the entire Bible.

Recognize the Different Types of Writing

The Bible is not a single book; it is a library. It contains many different types of literature, and we must read each type according to its own rules. You wouldn't read a book of poetry the same way you read a legal contract or a history textbook.

- **History:** Books like Genesis or Acts tell us what happened. They are records of real events.

- **Law:** Books like Leviticus give us God's commands for His people in a specific era.

- **Poetry and Psalms:** These use metaphors and emotions to express truth. When the Bible says God has "wings," it is using a poetic picture of protection, not saying God is a bird.

- **Proverbs:** These are general principles for wise living, not guaranteed promises for every single situation.

- **Letters:** These are direct instructions for churches and individuals.

Recognizing the "genre" or style of a book helps us avoid literalism where the author intended a figure of speech, and avoids turning history into mere symbols.

Use the Literal and Natural Meaning

Usually, the best way to understand a verse is to take it in its plain, literal sense. If the Bible tells a story of Jesus walking on water, it means He actually walked on water. We should not look for "secret" or "mystical" meanings behind every word.

However, taking the Bible literally also means recognizing when the author is using a figure of speech. When Jesus says, "I am the door," He is not saying He is made of wood and has hinges. He is saying He is the only way to enter God's kingdom. We use our common sense to see how the words were naturally intended to be understood.

Keep Christ at the Center

Jesus taught His disciples that the entire Old Testament pointed to Him (Luke 24:27). This is a vital key for interpretation. Whether we are reading about the temple sacrifices, the life of King David, or the warnings of the prophets, we should ask how these things lead us to Jesus.

The Bible is not just a list of rules or a collection of random stories. It is one grand story of God redeeming His people through Christ. If our interpretation of a passage doesn't eventually point us toward the person and work of Jesus, we have likely missed the main point.

Approach the Word With Humility

Interpretation is not just a mental exercise; it is a spiritual one. We need the help of the Holy Spirit to understand spiritual truth. Paul wrote that the natural person does not accept the things of the Spirit of God because they are spiritually discerned (1 Corinthians 2:14).

This means we must come to the Bible with a humble heart. We don't come as judges over the Word; we come as students under the Word. If we find something in the Bible that challenges our lifestyle or our opinions, we are the ones who must change, not the Bible. Humility means being willing to admit when we were wrong.

Read With the Church

While every believer can and should read the Bible for themselves, we do not read it by ourselves. We belong to a global and historical community of believers.

It is dangerous to come up with a "brand new" interpretation of a verse that no one in the last 2,000 years of church history has ever seen. We should listen to the wisdom of teachers, pastors, and the creeds we discussed in Chapter 4. Reading with the church helps keep us from falling into private errors or weird theories.

The Goal Is Not Just Information

The point of interpreting the Bible correctly is not just to win an argument or look smart. The goal is transformation. James warns us not to be just hearers of the Word, but doers also (James 1:22).

If you spend an hour studying the Greek grammar of a verse but it doesn't lead you to love God or your neighbor more, your study has failed. Proper interpretation leads to proper application. We interpret the Word so that we can live the Word.

Weekly Belief Statement

We believe that the Bible must be interpreted carefully, looking at the literal meaning, the historical context, and the overall message of Scripture. We believe that the Holy Spirit helps us understand God's Word as we approach it with humility. We hold that the central theme of all Scripture is the person and work of Jesus Christ.

Practical Application

✝ **Check the Context:** Pick a famous "promise" verse this week, like Jeremiah 29:11 or Philippians 4:13. Read the entire chapter around it. How does the context change or deepen your understanding of that verse?

✝ **Identify the Style:** Open your Bible to three random places. Identify what type of writing each one is (history, poetry, letter, etc.). How does the style change the way you should apply it?

✝ **Ask the "Christ Question":** As you do your daily reading this week, ask: "How does this passage show me my need for Jesus, or show me something beautiful about Jesus?"

✝ **Pray for Guidance:** Before you open your Bible, spend one minute in silence. Ask the Holy Spirit to remove your biases and help you see what the text actually says.

✝ **Read a Commentary:** If you find a passage confusing, look up what a trusted Christian teacher has said about it. See how their interpretation compares to your own.

"Think over what I say, for the Lord will give you understanding in everything" (2 Timothy 2:7).

PART THREE
Know the Living God

CHAPTER 9
Worship the One True God

The first step in knowing God is admitting that there is only one of Him. This sounds simple, but it is the most important truth in the universe. In the ancient world, people lived in fear of many gods. They thought one god ruled the sea, another ruled the harvest, and another ruled the sun. They spent their lives trying to please all of them at once.

Today, most people do not bow down to statues of stone. However, many still live as if there are many "gods" to serve. They divide their loyalty between money, career, comfort, and self. This chapter explores the foundational truth that there is only one God. He is the Creator, the Sustainer, and the rightful King of everything. When we worship the one true God, our lives find their proper focus.

The Great Commandment

For thousands of years, the Jewish people have started their day with a prayer called the *Shema*. It comes from Deuteronomy 6:4: "Hear, O Israel: The Lord our God, the Lord is one." This was not just a religious slogan. It was a declaration of reality.

In a world full of idols, Israel was called to be different. They were to serve one Master. This truth protected them from the chaos of trying to please multiple deities. It also gave them a sense of unity. Because there is only one God, there is only one source of truth and one ultimate authority.

Jesus called this the most important commandment of all. He added that we should love this one God with all our heart, soul, mind, and strength. If there were many gods, our love would be divided. Because there is only one, we can give Him everything.

God Is Distinct From His Creation

One of the most important things to understand about the one true God is that He is not part of the world. Some people believe that God is the universe, or that everything is God. This is called pantheism. Others believe that God is a force that lives inside every tree and rock.

The Bible teaches something different. God made the world, but He is separate from it. He existed before the mountains were brought forth. He is not a "piece" of nature; He is the Architect of nature.

This matters because it means God is not limited by the world. He does not get tired. He does not change with the seasons. He is the "I AM," the one who exists on His own. Because He is distinct from the world, He has the power to rule over it and the authority to judge it.

The Vanity of Idols

The Bible often uses humor and sharp language to describe idols. The prophets pointed out how foolish it is to cut down a tree, use half of it for firewood, and carve the other half into a god (Isaiah 44:14-17). An idol has eyes but cannot see. It has ears but cannot hear. It has to be carried because it cannot walk.

An idol is anything that takes the place of God in your heart. It is anything you look to for ultimate security, identity, or happiness. The problem with idols is not just that they are wrong; it is that they are weak. They cannot save you when life gets hard. They cannot offer you forgiveness. They cannot give you eternal life. Only the one true God can do those things.

God Is Jealous for His Glory

In our culture, we often think of jealousy as a bad thing. It usually means we are insecure or want something that belongs to someone else. But God's jealousy is different. It is a holy jealousy. It is the protective love of a husband for his wife.

God knows that He is the best thing for us. He knows that when we worship other things, we are hurting ourselves. He demands our exclusive worship because He alone deserves it. To give worship to anything else is to believe a lie. When God says, "You shall have no other gods before me," He is protecting us from the emptiness of false worship.

One God for All Nations

Because there is only one God, He is the God of all people. He is not a local god for one specific country or culture. He is the King of all the earth. This is why Christians are called to share the gospel with every nation.

If there were many gods, then different religions might all be "true" for different people. But if there is only one God who created the stars and breathed life into every human, then everyone needs to know Him. The oneness of God is the reason for the mission of the church. We invite everyone to turn from their local idols to serve the living and true God.

Living in the Presence of the One

Knowing there is only one God changes your daily perspective. It simplifies your life. Instead of trying to please everyone around you, you focus on pleasing your Creator. You don't have to wonder who is in charge of your future. The same God who rules the galaxies is the same God who counts the hairs on your head.

This truth also provides a ground for peace. When the world feels chaotic, we remember that there is not a war between many equal gods. There is only one Almighty God, and His purposes will stand. No other power in the universe can challenge Him. When you belong to the one true God, you are on the winning side.

Worshiping the True God

True worship is not just singing songs on Sunday. It is a life of "counting God as worthy." It means acknowledging His place as the center of everything.

We worship God by listening to His Word. We worship Him by obeying His commands, even when it is hard. We worship Him by trusting His character when we don't understand our circumstances. Most of all, we worship Him by enjoying Him. When we find our greatest joy in God, we show the world that He is better than any idol.

Weekly Belief Statement

We believe in the one true and living God, the Creator of all things. We believe He is distinct from His creation and sovereign over all the earth. We reject all forms of idolatry and confess that God alone is worthy of our ultimate love, trust, and worship.

Practical Application

Identify the Rivals: Take five minutes today to ask yourself: "What is the one thing I am most afraid of losing?" Often, our greatest fears reveal our "other gods." Bring that thing to God and tell Him He is more important.

Simplify Your Focus: When you feel overwhelmed this week, stop and say the words: "The Lord is one." Remind yourself that you only have one ultimate Master to please.

Practice Gratitude: List five things you enjoy (like coffee, a friend, or a sunset). Practice thanking the one true God for them, acknowledging that He is the Source of every good thing.

Read the First Commandment: Read Exodus 20:1-6. Reflect on why God starts His law by establishing who He is.

Observe Nature: Look at the complexity of the world. Remind yourself that this did not happen by accident or by a committee of gods. One brilliant Mind designed it all.

"Hear, O Israel: The Lord our God, the Lord is one. You shall love the Lord your God with all your heart and with all your soul and with all your might"
(Deuteronomy 6:4-5).

CHAPTER 10
Praise God for His Greatness

When we think about God, we often start with how He helps us or how He feels about us. While those things are important, theology must first look at God as He is in Himself. Before the world was made, God was already great. He does not need us to be God, but we need Him for every breath we take.

This chapter looks at the attributes of God that belong to Him alone. These are often called His "incommunicable" attributes because He does not share them with us. We are not all-powerful, and we are not eternal. By looking at God's greatness, we find a reason to worship that goes far beyond our own feelings. We find a God who is big enough to handle our problems because He is bigger than the universe itself.

God Exists on His Own

The first thing to understand about God's greatness is that He is "self-existent." This means God does not depend on anyone or anything for His existence. Humans need food, water, air, and a Creator. God needs nothing. He has life in Himself.

When Moses asked God for His name, God replied, "I AM WHO I AM" (Exodus 3:14). This name tells us that God simply is. He has no beginning and no end. He was not born, and He cannot die. He is the only Being in the universe who is completely independent.

This is good news for us. If God needed us, He would be as fragile as we are. But because He is self-sufficient, He is a rock that never moves. He gives to everyone life and breath and everything else, but He never needs to receive anything from us (Acts 17:25).

God Does Not Change

We live in a world where everything changes. Technology becomes old. Seasons turn from summer to winter. Our own bodies grow and age. Even our best friends can change their minds or their loyalties. But God is "immutable," which means He does not change.

Malachi 3:6 says, "For I the Lord do not change; therefore you, O children of Jacob, are not consumed." God's character, His promises, and His truth are the same today as they were thousands of years ago. He does not learn new facts that change His plans. He does not get "better" or "worse" over time.

Because God does not change, we can trust His Word. If He said He loves His people in the Bible, He still loves them today. If He promised to forgive those who repent, that promise still stands. His unchangeable nature is the anchor for our souls in a shifting world.

God Is All-Powerful

The greatness of God is seen in His "omnipotence," or His infinite power. There is nothing that is too hard for the Lord. He created the billions of stars in the sky just by speaking a word. He rules over the winds and the waves. He has power over life and death.

God's power is not just a raw force; it is a holy power used for His good purposes. He has the power to keep His promises. He has the power to change a human heart. He has the power to bring good out of a bad situation. When we feel weak, we do not have to find strength in ourselves. We look to the God who never gets tired and whose power has no limit.

God Knows Everything

God is "omniscient," meaning He has perfect and total knowledge. He does not have to research or investigate. He knows the past, the present, and the future perfectly. He knows the secrets of the deep ocean and the furthest corners of space.

Most importantly, God knows your heart. He knows your thoughts before you speak them. He knows your fears and your hidden hopes. For some, this might feel scary. But for those who trust Him, it is a comfort. You never have to explain yourself to God. He understands you better than you understand yourself. He knows your needs before you even ask Him for help.

God Is Everywhere at Once

God is "omnipresent." This means He is not limited by space or location. You cannot go anywhere where God is not already there. King David wrote in the Psalms that even if he went to the depths of the sea or the highest heavens, God would be there (Psalm 139:7-10).

This does not mean that God is "part" of the trees or the air. It means that His presence fills all of creation. He is fully present in a church in Africa and fully present in a home in America at the very same moment. You are never alone. Whether you are in a hospital room, a crowded city, or a lonely desert, God is with you.

God Is Eternal

God exists outside of time. We are stuck in the "now," and we remember the "then." But God sees all of history at once. He is the Alpha and the Omega, the Beginning and the End. He was there at the start of time, and He will be there when time as we know it ends.

Because God is eternal, He is never in a hurry. He is never late. He works according to His eternal timing. When we feel like life is moving too fast or that we are running out of time, we can rest in the God who holds eternity in His hand. He has plenty of time for you.

The Greatness of God Produces Fear and Joy

When we truly see how great God is, it should produce a sense of "holy fear." This is not the fear of a slave for a cruel master. It is the awe and wonder of a person standing on the edge of the Grand Canyon. It is the realization that God is holy, vast, and mighty.

But this greatness also produces joy. Why? Because this great God is also our Father. The same God who sustains the orbits of the planets is the one who cares for you. If God were small, He couldn't help us. If He were just like us, He couldn't save us. It is His very greatness that makes Him a worthy object of our trust.

Stop Trying to Be God

One of the biggest causes of stress in our lives is trying to have God's attributes. We try to know everything (omniscience). We try to be everywhere at once (omnipresence). We try to control everything (omnipotence). We try to stay young forever (immutability).

Theology tells us to stop. We are the creatures; He is the Creator. We are allowed to be small because He is great. We are allowed to be weak because He is strong. When we acknowledge God's greatness, we find the freedom to be human. We can let go of the steering wheel and trust the One who truly rules the world.

Weekly Belief Statement

We believe that God is infinite in His greatness. He is self-existent, eternal, and unchangeable. He is all-powerful, all-knowing, and present everywhere. We believe that His greatness is beyond our full understanding and that He alone deserves our highest praise and total trust.

Practical Application

✝ **Acknowledge Your Limits:** At the end of the day, say a prayer like this: "Lord, I am not God. I cannot control tomorrow. I cannot be everywhere. I leave the world in Your hands."

✝ **Observe the Stars:** Spend a few minutes looking at the night sky. Remind yourself that God knows every star by name. Let the vastness of space remind you of the vastness of God's power.

✝ **Trust His Knowledge:** When you feel misunderstood by others, find comfort in God's omniscience. Remind yourself that He sees your heart and knows the truth.

✝ **Rest in His Presence:** If you feel lonely this week, sit in silence for five minutes. Intentionally remind yourself that God is in the room with you. He is "omnipresent" and never leaves you.

✝ **Meditate on a Name:** Look up the name "El Shaddai" (God Almighty). Reflect on how God's power is used to provide for and protect His people.

"Great is the Lord, and greatly to be praised, and his greatness is unsearchable." - Psalm 145:3

CHAPTER 11
Praise God for His Goodness

In the last chapter, we looked at the greatness of God: His power, His knowledge, and His eternal nature. But greatness alone does not make someone worthy of our love. A king can be powerful but cruel. A genius can be brilliant but selfish. For us to truly trust God, we must know that His heart is good.

This chapter looks at what are often called God's "moral attributes." These are the qualities that describe His character. While things like all-powerfulness belong to God alone, He shares qualities like love, justice, and mercy with us. We are called to reflect His goodness to the world. Understanding God's goodness is the key to a life of gratitude rather than a life of fear.

God Is the Definition of Good

When we say something is "good," we usually mean it meets a certain standard. We say a meal is good because it tastes right, or a person is good because they follow the rules. But God does not follow a standard outside of Himself. He *is* the standard.

Psalm 34:8 says, "Oh, taste and see that the Lord is good!" This means that everything God does is consistent with His perfect character. He is the source of every good and perfect gift (James 1:17). There is no darkness in Him, no hidden motives, and no capacity for evil.

Because God is the source of goodness, we can trust His laws. His commands are not meant to ruin our fun; they are meant to lead us toward what is truly good for us. When we move away from God's design, we are moving away from goodness itself.

The Holiness of God

To understand God's goodness, we must first understand His holiness. Holiness means that God is "set apart." He is completely separate from sin and moral failure. He is pure light.

In the Bible, when people came close to the presence of God, they were often overwhelmed by His holiness. The prophet Isaiah cried out, "Woe is me!" when he saw the Lord. Holiness is the "beauty" of God's character. It is the reason He cannot tolerate evil.

Some people think holiness makes God distant or cold. But holiness is actually what makes His love so valuable. Because God is holy, His love is not a weak sentiment. It is a pure, committed, and honest love. He loves us enough to want us to be holy too.

God Is Love

The most famous description of God is found in 1 John 4:8: "God is love." This does not mean that love is god, but that love is the very essence of who God is. Before the world was made, the Father, Son, and Holy Spirit lived in a perfect relationship of love.

God's love is "agape" love. This is a choice to seek the highest good of another person, regardless of the cost. God did not love us because we were attractive or because we did something to earn it. He loved us because He is love.

The greatest proof of God's love is the cross. Romans 5:8 says that God shows His love for us in that while we were still sinners, Christ died for us. God's love is not a distant feeling; it is a sacrificial action. When you doubt if God cares for you, you don't look at your circumstances. You look at the cross.

God Is Just and Fair

Many people struggle to connect God's love with His justice. They think that if God is loving, He should just ignore sin. But a "good" judge who ignores crime is not actually good; he is corrupt. Because God is good, He must be just.

Justice means that God gives everyone exactly what they deserve. He stands up for the oppressed. He punishes the wicked. He maintains the moral order of the universe.

The beauty of the gospel is that at the cross, God's justice and His love met. God did not ignore sin; He punished it in Jesus so that He could be both "just and the justifier" of those who have faith (Romans 3:26). God's justice is our hope because it means that one day, every wrong will be made right.

God Is Merciful and Gracious

While justice is getting what you deserve, mercy is *not* getting the punishment you deserve. Grace is getting a gift you *don't* deserve. God is "abounding in steadfast love and faithfulness" (Exodus 34:6).

God's mercy means He is compassionate toward our weakness. He is patient with us when we fail. His grace means He pours out blessings on us, like forgiveness, adoption into His family, and eternal life, that we could never earn.

If God were only just, we would all be lost. If He were only merciful, He would not be holy. But because He is perfectly good, He is both. He offers us grace through the work of Christ, inviting us to come to Him just as we are.

The Faithfulness of God

Another part of God's goodness is His faithfulness. This means God always keeps His word. He never breaks a promise. He never changes His mind about His people.

We live in a world of broken promises. People change their minds, they forget, or they simply fail. But God is a "covenant-keeping" God. Lamentations 3:22-23 tells us that His mercies are new every morning and "great is your faithfulness." You can build your life on His promises because He is the only One who is 100% reliable.

Goodness in the Middle of Pain

The hardest time to believe in God's goodness is when we are suffering. We ask, "If God is good, why is this happening?" It is important to remember that God's goodness is not defined by our comfort.

A surgeon is good even when he has to use a knife to remove a tumor. A father is good even when he says "no" to his child for their safety. In the same way, God often uses difficult things to produce a greater good in us. We may not see the "why" right now, but we can trust the "Who." Because we know God's character is good, we can trust Him even when the path is dark.

Responding to God's Goodness

Knowing that God is good should change how we live. First, it should lead us to repentance. Romans 2:4 says that God's kindness is meant to lead us to turn away from sin. When we see how good He is, we realize how foolish it is to disobey Him.

Second, it should lead us to be content. If God is good and He is in control, then we have everything we need. We don't have to be jealous of others or anxious about the future.

Finally, it should lead us to be good to others. As followers of God, we are His ambassadors. We are called to be merciful, just, and loving because our Father is merciful, just, and loving. When we show goodness to our neighbors, we are showing them a small reflection of the living God.

Weekly Belief Statement

We believe that God is perfectly good in His nature and in all His works. We believe He is holy, just, and faithful. We confess that God is love and that He shows His goodness through His mercy and grace toward sinners. We believe that His goodness is the foundation of our trust and the reason for our praise.

Practical Application

- **Practice Gratitude:** Every evening this week, write down three "good gifts" you received that day. Acknowledge God as the source of those gifts.

- **Reflect on the Cross:** Spend fifteen minutes reading the story of the crucifixion (such as Mark 15). Remind yourself that this is the ultimate proof of God's love and justice.

- **Act With Mercy:** Identify someone this week who has annoyed you or let you down. Intentionally show them mercy or kindness instead of "getting even."

- **Study a Promise:** Find one promise of God in the Bible (like Matthew 28:20 or Hebrews 13:5). Meditate on God's faithfulness to keep that promise to you personally.

- **Trust in the Dark:** If you are facing a struggle, pray: "Lord, I don't understand this situation, but I know Your character is good. I trust Your heart even when I can't see Your hand."

"The Lord is good to all, and his mercy is over all that he has made." - Psalm 145:9

CHAPTER 12
Confess the Trinity With Joy

The doctrine of the Trinity is one of the most unique parts of the Christian faith. It is also one of the most misunderstood. Some people think it sounds like a math problem that does not add up. Others worry that it is a pagan idea that crept into the church. But the truth is that the Trinity is the heart of who God is. Without it, we would not have the gospel.

This chapter looks at the truth that God is one Being who exists eternally in three Persons: the Father, the Son, and the Holy Spirit. While the word "Trinity" is not in the Bible, the reality of it is on every page. We do not have to master every detail to worship God. We simply need to receive what He has said about Himself. When we confess the Trinity, we are invited into a relationship with the God who has lived in a perfect community of love forever.

One God, Three Persons

To understand the Trinity, we must hold two truths together at the same time. First, as we saw in Chapter 9, there is only one God. Christians are not polytheists. We do not believe in three gods. Second, the Bible clearly identifies the Father as God, the Son as God, and the Holy Spirit as God.

They are not three "parts" of God, like pieces of a pie. Each Person is fully and completely God. Yet, they are distinct from one another. The Father is not the Son. The Son is not the Spirit. The Spirit is not the Father.

This is a mystery because nothing in creation is exactly like it. Every analogy we try to use, like water, steam, and ice, usually ends up being wrong. Instead of trying to find a perfect picture, we should stick to what the Bible says. We worship one God in three Persons.

The Father Is God

The Bible begins by showing us God the Father as the Creator of all things. He is the source of all life and the one who initiates the plan of salvation. Jesus spoke often of His Father, teaching us to pray to Him and trust Him. The Father is the one who loved the world so much that He sent His Son.

Throughout the New Testament, the Father is praised as the "God and Father of our Lord Jesus Christ" (Ephesians 1:3). He is the Sovereign King who rules over history. Every good thing comes from His hand.

The Son Is God

Some people think Jesus was just a good teacher or a prophet. But the Bible says that Jesus is God in the flesh. John 1:1 says, "The Word was with God, and the Word was God." Jesus did things that only God can do. He forgave sins, He calmed the storm with a word, and He rose from the dead.

Jesus also claimed to be one with the Father. He said, "I and the Father are one" (John 10:30). He did not mean they were the same Person, but that they share the same divine nature. Because Jesus is God, His death on the cross has the power to save everyone who believes. Only a God-man could bridge the gap between us and the Father.

The Holy Spirit Is God

The Holy Spirit is not a "force" or an "it." He is a Person. He can be grieved, He speaks, and He makes choices. The Bible treats the Holy Spirit as fully divine. In the book of Acts, when a man lied to the Holy Spirit, Peter told him he had lied to God (Acts 5:3-4).

The Spirit is the one who applies the work of Jesus to our lives. He gives us new life, He comforts us, and He empowers us to live for God. Without the Holy Spirit, we would be left to try to follow God in our own strength. But because the Spirit is God dwelling within us, we have the power of God available to us every day.

The Trinity in the Story of Salvation

The best way to see the Trinity is to look at the work of salvation. The Father chose us before the foundation of the world. The Son came to earth to die for our sins. The Holy Spirit opens our eyes to see the truth and seals us for the day of redemption.

We see all three Persons together at the baptism of Jesus (Matthew 3:16-17). The Son is in the water. The Spirit descends like a dove. The

Father speaks from heaven, saying, "This is my beloved Son, with whom I am well pleased."

We also see the Trinity in how we are baptized. Jesus told His disciples to baptize "in the name of the Father and of the Son and of the Holy Spirit" (Matthew 28:19). Notice He said "name" (singular), not "names" (plural). This shows the unity of the three Persons in one Godhead.

Why the Trinity Matters for Your Life

You might wonder if this is just an abstract theory for theologians. It is not. The Trinity changes everything about how we live. First, it tells us that God is social and loving in His very nature. Because God has always existed as three Persons, love has always existed. God did not create us because He was lonely. He created us so that we could share in the love He already had.

Second, the Trinity gives us a pattern for community. Just as the Father, Son, and Spirit live in perfect harmony and mutual honor, we are called to live in unity with one another. We see that diversity and unity can go together.

Third, it changes how we pray. We pray to the Father, through the Son, by the help of the Holy Spirit. When you realize that the entire Trinity is involved in your life, your prayer life gains a new sense of depth and security.

Confess With Humility and Joy

We will never fully understand the Trinity in this life. That is okay. If we could explain God perfectly, He wouldn't be much of a God. We should be suspicious of any religion that makes God small enough to fit inside a human brain.

Instead of being frustrated by the mystery, we should be joyful. The Trinity means that God is far more beautiful and complex than we ever imagined. It means that the love we experience in this life is a small echo of the eternal love of God. We don't have to solve the mystery; we just have to worship the God who is there.

Trust the Revelation

Some people try to change the Trinity to make it easier to understand. They say God is like a man who is a father, a son, and a husband. This is an error because those are just "roles" one person plays. God is not one Person playing three roles; He is three distinct Persons.

We must be careful to stick to what the Bible reveals. We trust God's testimony about Himself. When we confess the Trinity, we are standing with the church throughout history. We are declaring that we believe in the God who has made Himself known as our Creator, our Redeemer, and our Sanctifier.

Weekly Belief Statement

We believe in the one true and living God who exists eternally in three Persons: Father, Son, and Holy Spirit. We believe that each Person is fully God, sharing the same nature, attributes, and glory. We rejoice in the mystery of the Trinity and find our life and hope in the love of the Father, the grace of the Son, and the fellowship of the Spirit.

Practical Application

✝ **Pray Trinitarianly:** This week, consciously address each Person of the Trinity in your prayers. Thank the Father for His plan, the Son for His sacrifice, and the Spirit for His presence.

✝ **Read the Greeting:** Read 2 Corinthians 13:14. Reflect on how Paul uses all three Persons of the Trinity to bless the church.

✝ **Reject Simplistic Analogies:** When you hear people try to explain the Trinity with eggs or water, remind yourself that God is unique. Practice being comfortable with the mystery.

✝ **Study a Hymn:** Look up the lyrics to "Holy, Holy, Holy." Notice how it praises God as "Blessed Trinity" and "God in Three Persons."

✝ **Look for Unity:** Identify one area in your local church where there is division. Ask God how you can promote a unity that reflects the harmony of the Trinity.

"The grace of the Lord Jesus Christ and the love of God and the fellowship of the Holy Spirit be with you all." -
2 Corinthians 13:14

CHAPTER 13
Know the Father as Creator and Provider

When we think of a father, we often think of someone who gives life and then works to sustain it. In the same way, the first Person of the Trinity is known primarily as the Father. This title is not just a metaphor. It describes a deep reality. God the Father is the source of all things and the one who keeps all things running.

This chapter looks at the specific work of the Father. While the whole Trinity was involved in creation, the Bible often highlights the Father as the Architect of the universe. He is also the great Provider who cares for the birds of the air and the people in His image. When we know the Father, we find a sense of belonging and safety. We realize that we are not accidents drifting in a cold universe, but children in a house built by a loving Father.

The Father as the Source of All Life

The Bible begins with the Father bringing the world into existence. He is the "Father of lights" (James 1:17) and the Creator of every family in heaven and on earth. This means that everything we see, the stars, the oceans, and our own bodies, started as a thought in His mind.

Being the Creator means the Father has rights over the world. He owns it because He made it. He has the authority to set the rules and define the purpose of life. But His authority is not that of a tyrant. It is the authority of a Father who wants His creation to flourish. When we acknowledge the Father as Creator, we admit that we belong to Him.

The Father Who Plans Our Rescue

The Father is also the one who initiated the plan to save us. Before the world was even made, the Father loved us. He did not wait for us to ask for help. He took the lead.

In the story of salvation, the Father is the Sender. He sent the Son to be the Savior of the world (1 John 4:14). He is also the one who "predestined" us to be adopted as His children through Jesus Christ. This shows that our salvation is rooted in the Father's heart. He wanted a family, and He was willing to pay a great price to bring us home.

The Father as Our Daily Provider

One of the most comforting things Jesus taught was that the Father knows exactly what we need. In the Sermon on the Mount, Jesus told us not to be anxious about food or clothes. He pointed to the lilies of the field and the sparrows in the sky. If the Father takes care of them, how much more will He take care of you?

Providence is the word we use for God's ongoing care. The Father does not just "wind up" the world like a clock and walk away. He is actively involved. He sends the rain on the just and the unjust. He provides the air we breathe and the strength for our daily work.

When we pray "Give us this day our daily bread," we are acknowledging that every bite of food is a gift from the Father's hand. We stop looking at our bank accounts or our bosses as the ultimate source of our security. We look through them to the Father who uses them to provide for us.

The Father's Discipline and Care

A good father does more than just give gifts; he also provides direction and correction. The Bible says that the Lord disciplines the ones He loves (Hebrews 12:6). If we never faced challenges or consequences, we would never grow up.

The Father's discipline is never about anger or revenge. It is about training. He wants us to share in His holiness. When we go through hard times, we can trust that the Father is at work. He is not being cruel; He is being a Father. He is shaping us into the likeness of His Son, Jesus.

Access to the Father

In many religions, God is seen as a distant King who is hard to reach. But because of Jesus, we have direct access to the Father. We can call Him "Abba," which is a close, personal term like "Papa" or "Dad."

Romans 8:15 tells us that we have received the Spirit of adoption. We are no longer slaves who have to fear. We are sons and daughters who can run into the Father's presence at any time. This access is a gift. We don't have to perform well to get His attention. We don't have to be perfect to keep His love. We come to Him based on the work of Jesus.

Living as Children of the Father

Knowing the Father changes how we interact with the world. First, it kills our pride. If everything we have is a gift from the Father, we have nothing to boast about. We are simply beggars who have been invited to a King's table.

Second, it kills our anxiety. If the Creator of the universe is our Father, what is there to fear? Even the most powerful people in the world are just creatures under His hand. Nothing can happen to us that has not first passed through the Father's permission.

Third, it changes how we treat others. If God is the Father of all, then every human being has dignity. We are called to reflect the Father's generosity by being generous to those in need. We love because He first loved us.

The Father's Eternal House

The story of the Father ends with a homecoming. Jesus promised that in His Father's house are many rooms, and He has gone to prepare a place for us (John 14:2).

Our life on earth is just the beginning. We are heading toward an eternal relationship with the Father in a world where there will be no more tears, pain, or death. The Father who created us and provided for us in this life will be our joy forever in the next. Trusting the Father means living with your eyes on that future home.

Weekly Belief Statement

We believe in God the Father Almighty, Creator of heaven and earth. We believe He is the source of all life and the merciful Provider for all His creatures. We believe He has adopted us as His children through faith in Jesus Christ, and we trust in His wise providence, His loving discipline, and His eternal care.

Practical Application

- **Practice "Abba" Prayer:** This week, start your prayers by specifically calling God "Father" or "Abba." Spend a moment thinking about what it means to be His child before you ask for anything.

- **Observe the Providers:** Look at the natural world—the rain, the soil, the sun. Thank the Father for the way He provides for the earth without any help from us.

✝ **Release an Anxiety:** Identify one thing you are worried about today. Intentionally "hand it over" to the Father, reminding yourself that He knows your needs better than you do.

✝ **Read the Prodigal Son:** Read Luke 15:11-32. Focus on the character of the father in the story. How does his reaction to his son change your view of God the Father?

✝ **Give Generously:** Since your Father is a Provider, find a way to provide for someone else this week. Give a meal, a gift, or your time to someone in need as a way to reflect the Father's heart.

"See what kind of love the Father has given to us, that we should be called children of God; and so we are." -
1 John 3:1

CHAPTER 14
Follow the Son as Lord and Savior

If the Bible is a ring, then Jesus Christ is the diamond set at its center. All of human history leads up to Him, and all of eternity flows from Him. While the Father initiated our rescue, the Son is the one who stepped into our world to accomplish it. He is not just a character in a book or a distant historical figure. He is the living Lord.

This chapter looks at the second Person of the Trinity: God the Son. We will see how He left the glory of heaven to become one of us. We will look at His two greatest roles: Savior and Lord. To follow Jesus means more than just believing facts about Him. It means trusting His work to save you and submitting to His rule to lead you. When we follow the Son, we find the only path that leads back to the Father.

The Son Who Was Always There

Before Jesus was born in Bethlehem, He existed eternally as the Son of God. He did not begin His life in a manger. John's Gospel tells us that in the beginning was the Word, and the Word was with God, and the Word was God (John 1:1).

The Son was active in the creation of the world. He was the one who sustained the universe before He ever took a human breath. This is important because it means Jesus is not a "created" being. He is the Creator. When He came to earth, He didn't stop being God; He simply added a human nature to His divine nature. He became the God-man so that He could stand between God and man.

Jesus as Our Perfect Savior

The name "Jesus" literally means "The Lord saves." The primary reason the Son came to earth was to deal with the problem of sin. Because God is holy, sin must be punished. Because we are sinners, we cannot pay that debt ourselves and survive. We needed a substitute.

As our Savior, Jesus did two things. First, He lived the perfect life we could not live. He obeyed every law and honored the Father in every thought. Second, He died the death we deserved to die. On the cross, He took the weight of our guilt upon Himself. He paid the price in full.

When we call Jesus "Savior," we are admitting that we cannot save ourselves. We are stopping our efforts to be "good enough" and resting in what He has already done. His resurrection from the dead is the proof that His sacrifice was accepted. The grave is empty, and the debt is paid.

Jesus as Our Sovereign Lord

Following the Son involves more than just accepting a "fire insurance" policy for the afterlife. It means acknowledging Him as Lord. In the ancient world, "Lord" was a title for a king or a master. It meant someone who has the right to tell you what to do.

When we confess that "Jesus is Lord," we are handing over the keys to our lives. We are saying that His will matters more than our feelings. His word matters more than our opinions. His goals matter more than our comfort.

Many people want Jesus as a Savior but not as a Lord. They want the forgiveness of sins without the change of life. But the Bible does not give us that option. You cannot have the benefit of His death without the authority of His life. To follow Him is to move where He moves and love what He loves.

The Prophet, Priest, and King

Throughout history, the church has described Jesus using three specific offices. These help us understand how He works in our lives today.

- **Prophet:** As a Prophet, Jesus is the ultimate Word of God. He teaches us the truth about God and ourselves. We follow Him by listening to His voice in the Scriptures.

- **Priest:** As a Priest, Jesus represents us before the Father. He offered Himself as the final sacrifice, and now He lives to pray for us. We follow Him by coming to God with confidence, knowing Jesus is our Advocate.

- **King:** As a King, Jesus rules over His church and the whole world. He protects us and guides us. We follow Him by obeying His commands and serving His kingdom.

The Humility of the Son

The way Jesus lived on earth gives us a model for how to follow Him. Though He was the King of the universe, He was born in a stable. Though He was the source of all wealth, He had no place to lay His head. He washed the feet of His disciples, including the one who would betray Him.

Following the Son means adopting His heart of service. We cannot be proud followers of a humble Savior. If Jesus was willing to give up His rights for us, we must be willing to give up our rights for others. True greatness in His kingdom is found in being the servant of all.

The Return of the Son

The story of the Son is not over. After His resurrection, He ascended into heaven, but He promised to come back. He is coming again to judge the living and the dead and to set the world right.

This gives the follower of Jesus a great sense of hope. We do not have to fix everything in this world by our own power. We work hard, but we wait for the King to return and finish the work. Knowing He is coming back keeps us focused on what truly matters. It keeps us from getting too attached to the things of this world.

A Relationship, Not Just a Religion

At its core, following the Son is about a relationship. Jesus said, "My sheep hear my voice, and I know them, and they follow me" (John 10:27). He does not just want your religious performance; He wants your heart.

He knows your name. He knows your struggles. He invites you to walk with Him daily. This is the beauty of the gospel: the Son of God became a son of man so that the sons of men could become children of God.

Weekly Belief Statement

We believe in Jesus Christ, the eternal Son of God, who became man for our salvation. We believe He lived a perfect life, died on the cross for our sins, and rose again on the third day. We confess Him as our only Savior and our supreme Lord, and we commit to following Him in humility, obedience, and hope.

Practical Application

- **Audit Your Loyalties:** Ask yourself: "In which area of my life am I struggling to let Jesus be Lord?" (Is it your money, your time, your speech, or your relationships?) Commit that area to Him today.

✝ **Read a Gospel:** Spend time this week reading through the Gospel of Mark. Focus on the actions of Jesus. Pay attention to how He serves people and how He exercises His authority.

✝ **Practice Silence:** Take five minutes each morning to sit in silence and say, "Jesus, I am Your servant. What would You have me do today?" Listen for the principles of His Word in your heart.

✝ **Identify the "Cross" Moments:** When you face a situation where you want to be selfish, remember the sacrifice of Jesus. Choose to serve or give instead of taking, as an act of following Him.

✝ **Celebrate the Resurrection:** Remind yourself every morning this week: "Jesus is alive." Let that truth change your mood and give you energy for your tasks.

"If anyone would come after me, let him deny himself and take up his cross daily and follow me." - Luke 9:23

CHAPTER 15
Depend on the Holy Spirit as Helper and Guide

Many Christians feel like they are trying to live the Christian life on their own power. They have the rules, they have the Bible, and they have the example of Jesus, but they feel like an engine without any fuel. This is where the third Person of the Trinity comes in. The Holy Spirit is not a distant influence or a vague feeling. He is God with us and God in us.

This chapter looks at the vital work of the Holy Spirit. We will see how He brings us to life, how He teaches us the truth, and how He gives us the strength to follow Jesus. To live a fruitful life, we must move from trying to do things for God to letting God do things through us. When we depend on the Spirit, we find that the Christian life is not a heavy burden, but a life led by a powerful Helper.

The Person of the Holy Spirit

Before we look at what the Spirit does, we must remember who He is. As we discussed in Chapter 12, the Holy Spirit is a Person. He has a mind, emotions, and a will. He is fully God, equal in power and glory with the Father and the Son.

Jesus called the Spirit the "Paraclete," a Greek word that means "one called alongside to help." This was often used for a legal advocate or a Comforter. Jesus promised His disciples that even though He was leaving them physically, He would not leave them as orphans. He would send "another Helper" who would be with them forever (John 14:16). The Spirit is the presence of Jesus with us today.

The Spirit Gives New Life

Our relationship with the Spirit begins at the moment of our salvation. The Bible says that without the Spirit, we are spiritually dead. We cannot see the beauty of the gospel or choose to follow God on our own.

The Holy Spirit is the one who "convicts" us of sin. He opens our eyes to see our need for a Savior. Then, He performs the miracle of new birth. This is called regeneration. He takes a heart of stone and gives us a heart of flesh. Every bit of desire you have for God is a gift from the Holy Spirit. He is the one who puts the life of God into the soul of man.

The Spirit Is Our Teacher

One of the primary roles of the Spirit is to guide us into all truth (John 16:13). He is the one who inspired the writers of the Bible, and He is the one who helps us understand it today. This is called illumination.

Have you ever read a verse you had seen a hundred times before, but suddenly it made sense and touched your heart? That is the work of the Holy Spirit. He takes the words on the page and makes them "alive" to us. He reminds us of what Jesus taught and helps us apply it to our specific situations. When we are confused about a decision or a doctrine, we should ask the Spirit for clarity.

The Spirit Produces Fruit in Us

The goal of the Christian life is to become more like Jesus. This is not something we can force by sheer willpower. It is the natural result of the Spirit living in us. Paul calls this the "fruit of the Spirit" (Galatians 5:22-23).

This fruit includes love, joy, peace, patience, kindness, goodness, faithfulness, gentleness, and self-control. Notice that it is called "fruit," not "works." A tree does not struggle to grow an apple; it grows an apple by staying connected to the roots and the sun. In the same way, as we "abide" in Christ, the Spirit naturally produces these qualities in our character. If you find yourself lacking in patience or love, the answer is not just to "try harder," but to ask the Spirit to fill you more.

The Spirit Gives Gifts for Service

The Holy Spirit also gives "spiritual gifts" to every believer. These are special abilities given to help build up the church. Some are given the gift of teaching, others the gift of encouragement, and others the gift of service or leadership.

No one has every gift, and no one has no gift. We need each other. The Spirit distributes these gifts exactly as He chooses (1 Corinthians 12:11). The purpose of these gifts is never to make us look important. They are tools for us to use to love others and point people to Jesus. When you use your gift, you are acting as a channel for the Spirit's power.

How to Depend on the Spirit

Living by the Spirit is a daily choice. Paul uses the phrase "walk by the Spirit." Walking is a step-by-step process. It means staying in constant communication with Him throughout the day.

We depend on the Spirit by "quenching not" His influence. This means when we feel a nudge to pray, to help someone, or to turn away from a temptation, we listen. We also depend on Him through prayer and the Word. Since the Spirit wrote the Bible, He always works in harmony with it. He will never lead you to do something that contradicts the Scriptures.

When we fail and sin, we grieve the Spirit. But because He is our Helper, He is also the one who leads us back to repentance. He reminds us that we are still children of God and helps us get back on the path.

The Guarantee of Our Future

Finally, the Holy Spirit is described as a "seal" or a "guarantee" of our inheritance (Ephesians 1:13-14). In the ancient world, a seal was a mark of ownership and protection. Because the Spirit lives in you, you can be sure that you belong to God.

He is like a down payment on a house. His presence in your life today is a promise that God will finish the work He started. He is the "firstfruits" of the glory that is coming. When you feel weak or doubt your salvation, look at the evidence of the Spirit's work in your life. Even a small desire to please God is a sign that the Spirit is there, and He will never leave you.

Weekly Belief Statement

We believe in the Holy Spirit, the Lord and Giver of life. We believe He is the Helper promised by Jesus who dwells within every believer. We believe He convicts us of sin, leads us into truth, produces spiritual fruit in our character, and gives us gifts to serve the church. We commit to depending on His power rather than our own strength.

Practical Application

✝ **Ask for the Filling:** Every morning this week, pray: "Holy Spirit, I cannot live this day on my own. Please fill me, guide me, and give me Your strength."

✝ **Look for the Fruit:** Choose one "fruit of the Spirit" (like patience or gentleness) that you struggle with. Ask the Spirit to specifically produce that fruit in you during a difficult moment this week.

✝ **Listen for Nudges:** Pay attention to small "nudges" to do good—like sending a text to a friend or helping a neighbor. Practice acting on those nudges immediately as an exercise in following the Spirit.

✝ **Read the Spirit's Book:** Spend ten minutes reading Romans 8. Notice how many times the Spirit is mentioned and what He does for the believer.

✝ **Identify Your Gift:** Ask a mature Christian friend, "What do you see the Holy Spirit doing through me to help others?" Use their answer to think about how you can serve your church this month.

"If we live by the Spirit, let us also keep in step with the Spirit." - Galatians 5:25

CHAPTER 16
Rest in God's Wise Plan

Life often feels like a puzzle with missing pieces. We face unexpected job losses, health scares, or global crises that leave us wondering if anyone is actually in charge. If we believe that God is great and good, we must eventually ask: does He have a plan for all this? The answer found in Scripture is a resounding "yes."

This chapter looks at the "decree" or the eternal plan of God. We will see that God is not reacting to events as they happen. He is not a chess player waiting for the world to move so He can decide His next step. He is the Sovereign King who has a wise and perfect plan for everything. When we learn to rest in this plan, we find a peace that remains steady even when our circumstances are falling apart.

God's Plan Is Eternal

God's plan did not begin when you were born, or even when the world was created. The Bible teaches that God's purposes are eternal. Paul writes that God works all things according to the counsel of His will (Ephesians 1:11).

This plan includes everything from the rising of the sun to the salvation of your soul. Because God is outside of time, He sees the end from the beginning. His plan is not a "Plan B" that He came up with after Adam and Eve sinned. It is a "Plan A" that was set in stone before the foundation of the world. This gives us immense security. Our lives are not subject to random luck or cold fate; they are held within an ancient, loving design.

The Wisdom of the Plan

One of the most important things to remember about God's plan is that it is wise. Sometimes we look at the world and think we could do a better job. We think we know who should be healthy, who should be wealthy, and how history should go. But our perspective is like looking at a single thread on the back of a massive tapestry.

God sees the whole picture. Romans 11:33 exclaims, "Oh, the depth of the riches and wisdom and knowledge of God! How unsearchable are his judgments and how inscrutable his ways!" God's wisdom means He chooses the best possible goals and the best possible ways to reach them. Even when His plan involves path we wouldn't choose, we can trust that His "map" is better than ours.

God Is Sovereign Over All Things

To say God has a plan is to say He is sovereign. Sovereignty means that God has the power and the right to do what He pleases. Nothing can thwart His purposes. Job admitted to God, "I know that you can do all things, and that no purpose of yours can be thwarted" (Job 42:2).

This sovereignty extends to the smallest details. Jesus said that not even a sparrow falls to the ground apart from the Father's will. It also extends to the largest events. God raises up leaders and brings them down. He sets the boundaries of nations. Even the heart of a king is like a stream of water in the hand of the Lord; He turns it wherever He will (Proverbs 21:1). Knowing God is sovereign means we don't have to live in fear of the "what-ifs."

Our Responsibility Within the Plan

A common question arises: if God has a plan for everything, does it matter what I do? Does human choice still count? The Bible answers with a clear "yes" to both. This is one of the great mysteries of the faith. God is 100% sovereign, and we are 100% responsible for our choices.

God does not treat us like robots. He uses our prayers, our decisions, and our actions to bring about His plan. We are called to obey His commands and make wise choices. We don't use "God's plan" as an excuse to be lazy or sinful. Instead, knowing God has a plan gives us the courage to act. We do our part, and we leave the results to Him.

The Ultimate Goal: God's Glory

What is the "point" of God's plan? Many people think the plan is mainly about making us happy. While God does care for our joy, the ultimate goal of His plan is His own glory. He works so that the whole universe will see how great, wise, and good He is.

This is actually the best thing for us. If the plan were centered on us, it would be as small and fragile as we are. But because the plan is centered on God's glory, it is as stable and magnificent as He is. When we align our lives with His glory, we find our highest purpose. We stop asking, "How can I get what I want?" and start asking, "How can God be honored in this situation?"

Resting in the Plan During Suffering

The hardest time to rest in God's plan is when we are in pain. When we lose a loved one or face a tragedy, "God's plan" can feel like a cold phrase. But it is in these moments that we need this truth the most.

The greatest example of this is the cross of Jesus. From a human perspective, the crucifixion was a terrible mistake and a great injustice. But the book of Acts tells us that Jesus was delivered up according to the "definite plan and foreknowledge of God" (Acts 2:23). God took the worst event in history and used it to bring about the best thing: our salvation. If God can bring the greatest good out of the death of His Son, He can bring good out of your trials too.

How to Rest

Resting is an active choice. It means consciously stopping our attempts to control the world. It means "letting go" of the anxiety that comes from trying to play God.

We rest by preaching the truth to ourselves. When we feel panicked, we remind ourselves: "God is in control. He is wise. He loves me. Nothing is catching Him by surprise." We also rest through prayer. We bring our requests to Him, and then we trust Him with the answer, knowing that if He says "no" or "wait," it is because He has a better plan that we cannot see yet.

A Plan for Good

The Bible gives us a beautiful promise about God's plan for His people. Romans 8:28 says that for those who love God, all things work together for good. This does not say that all things *are* good. It says they *work together* for good.

Think of a cake. Flour, raw eggs, and baking powder don't taste good on their own. In fact, they might make you sick. But when a master baker mixes them and puts them in the heat, the result is delicious. God is the Master Baker. He takes the bitter and the sweet parts of your life and blends them into something beautiful.

Weekly Belief Statement

We believe that God has an eternal and unchangeable plan for all things, which He carries out according to His perfect wisdom and for His own glory. We believe that God is sovereign over all events, yet He holds us responsible for our actions. We rest in the truth that God works all things together for the good of those who love Him and are called according to His purpose.

Practical Application

✝ **Look for the "Threads":** Think of a difficult time in your past. Can you now see how God used that situation to grow your character or lead you to a new opportunity? Thank Him for His hidden wisdom.

✝ **Release the Reins:** Identify one situation this week that you have been trying to control with worry. Say this prayer: "Lord, I give this to You. I trust Your plan more than my own."

✝ **Study the Cross:** Read Acts 4:24-28. Notice how the early church prayed by acknowledging God's sovereign plan even in the middle of persecution.

✝ **Practice Patience:** When you face a delay this week (like a long line or a traffic jam), instead of getting frustrated, remind yourself: "God is sovereign over my time. Maybe He has a reason for this delay."

✝ **Memorize the Promise:** Write out Romans 8:28 and put it where you will see it daily. Let it be the first thing you think of when things don't go your way.

"And we know that for those who love God all things work together for good, for those who are called according to his purpose." - Romans 8:28

PART FOUR
See God's World and Your Place in It

CHAPTER 17
Affirm That God Created All Things

Every story has a beginning. If we want to understand who we are and why we are here, we must go back to the very first sentence of the Bible: "In the beginning, God created the heavens and the earth" (Genesis 1:1). This is not just a statement about history. It is the foundation for our entire worldview. It tells us that the world is not an accident, and we are not the products of random chance.

This chapter looks at the act of creation. We will see that God made everything from nothing, that He did it by His powerful word, and that He did it for His own glory. When we affirm that God is the Creator, we find a sense of order and purpose. We realize that the world belongs to Him, and we are guests in His house.

Creation Out of Nothing

The Bible teaches that before the world began, only God existed. There was no "stuff" or pre-existing matter that He used to build the universe. In theology, we call this *creatio ex nihilo*, which is Latin for "creation out of nothing."

This is important because it shows God's absolute power. Humans can "create" things by rearranging what already exists. A carpenter makes a chair from wood, and an artist makes a painting from pigment. But only God can bring something out of nothing. By His mere will, He brought space, time, and matter into existence.

Because God made everything from nothing, He is the source of all that exists. Everything depends on Him. If He were to stop sustaining the world for even a second, everything would vanish. This humbles us and reminds us that we are completely dependent on our Creator for every breath.

The Power of God's Word

How did God create? He did not use tools or heavy machinery. He spoke. Throughout the first chapter of Genesis, we see the phrase, "And God said." When God speaks, reality happens. He said, "Let there be light," and there was light.

This shows the authority of God's Word. His voice carries the power to give life and set boundaries. If His word is powerful enough to create a galaxy, it is powerful enough to change your life. This is why we trust the Bible. The same God who spoke the world into being has spoken to us in His Word. When we listen to Him, we are listening to the One who defines reality.

Creation Is an Act of the Trinity

While we often associate creation with the Father, the Bible shows that the entire Trinity was involved. Genesis 1 mentions the Spirit of God hovering over the waters. John 1 tells us that through the Son (the Word), all things were made.

Creation was a team effort, so to speak. The Father planned it, the Son executed it, and the Spirit sustained it. This means the world bears the mark of the Trinity. It is full of diversity and unity. It reflects the beauty and harmony of the three Persons in one God. When we look at the world, we aren't just seeing a machine; we are seeing a masterpiece of the triune God.

God Is Distinct From Creation

Some people believe that God is the world or that the world is a part of God. This is a mistake. The Bible teaches that God is "transcendent," meaning He is completely separate from and above what He has made. The Creator is not the creature.

If God were part of the world, He would be limited by it. He would be subject to the same decay and change that we see in nature. But because He is the Creator, He rules over it. He is not "trapped" in the universe. He is the King who sits on a throne outside of time and space. This gives us hope because it means God has the power to step into His creation to save and help us.

The Purpose of Creation

Why did God bother to make the world? He did not make it because He was lonely or because He needed something. As we saw in earlier chapters, God is perfectly happy within Himself. He made the world to display His glory.

The heavens declare the glory of God (Psalm 19:1). Every mountain, every insect, and every distant star is a finger pointing back to the Creator. The world is like a giant theater designed to show off God's wisdom, power, and beauty. When we enjoy a beautiful sunset or marvel at the complexity of the human eye, we are supposed to say, "How great is the God who made this!"

Creation and the Order of Life

Because God created the world, the world has an inherent order. It is not a chaotic mess. There are laws of physics, laws of logic, and moral laws. God designed the world to work in a specific way.

When we follow God's design, life works better. When we ignore His design, we face friction and pain. Affirming God as Creator means we look to Him to see how life should be lived. We don't try to reinvent reality or make up our own truth. We submit to the Order-Giver. This brings a sense of peace because we realize that the world is not falling apart; it is being held together by the same Hand that made it.

The Rejection of Chance

Many people today are taught that the world is the result of a "cosmic accident." They believe that if you wait long enough, order will eventually come from chaos. But the Bible tells a different story. It tells us that a brilliant Mind intended for you to be here.

Believing in creation changes how you see yourself. You are not a random collection of cells. You are a work of art. You were made on purpose, for a purpose. This gives every human life infinite value. Whether someone is young or old, healthy or sick, they carry the dignity of being a creature made by God.

A New Creation Is Coming

The story of creation does not end with Genesis. Because of sin, the current creation is "groaning" and broken. But God has promised to make all things new. Through the work of Jesus, God is starting a "new creation."

If you are in Christ, you are a new creation already (2 Corinthians 5:17). And one day, the physical world will be renewed. There will be a new heaven and a new earth. The same God who spoke the first world into being will speak the final world into being. Trusting God as Creator means looking forward to the day when all the brokenness of this world is finally fixed.

Weekly Belief Statement

We believe that in the beginning, God created the heavens and the earth out of nothing by the power of His Word. We believe that the triune God is the source of all life and that His creation is distinct from Himself. We affirm that the world was made for His glory and that every part of it reflects His wisdom and power.

Practical Application

- **Look for the Fingerprints:** This week, find one thing in nature that amazes you. Spend five minutes thinking about the wisdom it took to design that specific thing. Thank God for His creativity.

- **Practice Dependency:** Every time you take a deep breath today, remind yourself: "I didn't make this air, and I didn't make these lungs. God did." Let it produce a heart of gratitude.

- **Respect the Design:** Think of one of God's commands that you find difficult. Remind yourself that the Creator knows how His world works better than you do. Choose to trust His "user manual" over your own feelings.

- **Read the Story:** Read Genesis chapter 1 and 2 this week. Pay attention to how often God speaks and how He brings order out of the darkness.

- **Honor Others:** Remind yourself that every person you meet today, even the ones who bother you, is a creature made by God. Treat them with the respect that their Creator deserves.

"Worthy are you, our Lord and God, to receive glory and honor and power, for you created all things, and by your will they existed and were created." - Revelation 4:11

CHAPTER 18
See Creation as Good and Purposeful

In the previous chapter, we affirmed that God is the Creator of all things. However, knowing *that* God created the world is only the beginning. We must also understand the *nature* of what He made. Some people view the physical world as a distraction from spiritual things, or even as something inherently evil. Others see it as a collection of random resources to be used however we please.

This chapter explores the biblical truth that God's creation is both inherently good and intentionally purposeful. When God finished His work, He did not just call it "finished"; He called it "very good" (Genesis 1:31). Understanding the goodness and purpose of creation changes how we treat our bodies, how we view our work, and how we care for the world around us.

The Goodness of the Material World

From the very first chapter of the Bible, God repeatedly pauses to declare that what He has made is "good" (Genesis 1:4, 10, 12, 18, 21, 25). This means that matter—the physical stuff of the universe—is not a mistake or a lower form of existence.

Some early false teachers suggested that only spiritual things were good and that physical bodies were "prisons" for the soul. The Bible rejects this. Because a good God created the physical world, the world itself is a gift to be enjoyed with gratitude. We see this in how God provided food, beauty, and companionship for humanity. When we enjoy a meal or a walk in the woods, we are experiencing the goodness of God's handiwork.

Creation Is a Revelation

Creation is not silent; it is a "natural revelation" of who God is. Psalm 19:1 tells us, "The heavens declare the glory of God, and the sky above proclaims his handiwork." Everything in nature acts as a mirror reflecting the attributes of the Creator.

The vastness of the ocean speaks of His power. The intricate design of a leaf speaks of His wisdom. The changing seasons speak of His faithfulness. Because creation is purposeful, we can learn about God by paying attention to what He has made. While creation cannot tell us the specific details of the gospel—which requires the Written Word—it leaves every person without excuse because God's "eternal power and divine nature" are clearly perceived in the things that have been made (Romans 1:20).

Humanity's Purpose: To Rule and Care

God did not create the world to be a museum that is never touched. He created it to be a home for humanity, and He gave us a specific purpose within it. In Genesis 1:28, God gave what is often called the "Cultural Mandate." He told humanity to "be fruitful and multiply and fill the earth and subdue it."

This means humanity was designed to be God's "sub-creators." We are called to take the raw materials of the world—the soil, the minerals, the sounds, and the ideas—and develop them into culture, art, technology, and community that honor God. Our work is not a result of the Fall; it was part of the original, "very good" purpose of creation. We find our purpose when we use our creativity to bring order and beauty out of the world God provided.

The Integrity of Design

Because creation is purposeful, it has an "integrity of design." This means things have a nature and a way they are meant to function. God set boundaries for the sea and rhythms for the day and night. He designed marriage and family. He designed our bodies to need rest and nourishment.

Living a purposeful life means respecting these designs. We are not free to redefine reality according to our own whims because we did not create reality. When we live in harmony with God's design, we experience the "shalom" (peace and wholeness) that He intended. When we fight against His design, we inevitably face brokenness.

Creation and the Incarnation

The ultimate proof of the goodness of creation is the Incarnation— when God the Son became a human being. If the physical world were evil or unimportant, God would never have taken on a physical body.

By becoming man, Jesus Christ "sanctified" (set apart as holy) human life and the physical world. He used water to baptize, bread and wine to signify His body and blood, and His own physical hands to heal the sick. The gospel is not about escaping the physical world to live as ghosts; it is about the redemption of the whole person—body and soul—and the eventual renewal of the whole creation.

Caring for God's Property

If the earth is the Lord's and everything in it (Psalm 24:1), then we are stewards, not owners. A steward is someone who manages another person's property according to the owner's wishes.

Our purpose includes "stewardship" of the environment. We do not worship nature, but we respect it because it belongs to our Father. We should not be wasteful or destructive because everything we touch is a gift from the Creator. Caring for creation is an act of worship because it honors the Maker of the world.

Creation Groaning for Renewal

We must acknowledge that the world we see now is not exactly as God first made it. Because of human sin, the ground was "cursed," and the creation was subjected to "futility" (Romans 8:20-22). We see this in natural disasters, disease, and death.

However, the Bible says that creation is "groaning" in expectation. It is waiting for the day when it will be set free from its bondage to decay. God's purpose for creation is not its destruction, but its transformation. Just as Jesus rose with a physical but glorified body, God has promised a "new heaven and a new earth" where righteousness dwells. Our hope is not just a "heavenly" existence, but a restored creation.

Weekly Belief Statement

We believe that God's creation is inherently good and filled with divine purpose. We affirm that the physical world is a gift from God and a revelation of His glory. We believe that humanity has been given the purposeful task of stewarding the earth and its resources for God's honor. We look forward with hope to the day when the groaning creation will be fully renewed in the new heaven and the new earth.

Practical Application

✝ **Notice the "Very Good":** This week, find three physical things you usually take for granted (like the taste of your favorite fruit, the feeling of the sun, or the ability to walk) and specifically thank God for their "goodness."

✠ **Work with Purpose:** Whatever your job or daily task is this week, do it as an act of "sub-creation." Ask yourself: "How am I bringing order, beauty, or help to God's world through this work?"

✠ **Practice Stewardship:** Identify one way you can be a better steward of God's physical world this week—perhaps by reducing waste, caring for a plant, or cleaning up a local space.

✠ **Reflect on Design:** Spend time reading Psalm 104. Note how God provides for every creature and how every part of nature has a specific place and role.

✠ **Treat Your Body with Respect:** Remind yourself that your body is a "good" creation of God. Choose one habit this week (like better sleep or healthy eating) that honors the physical design God gave you.

"For everything created by God is good, and nothing is to be rejected if it is received with gratitude". -
1 Timothy 4:4

CHAPTER 19
Trust God's Providence in Daily Life

In the previous chapters, we saw that God is the Creator who made all things "very good" and with a specific purpose. However, God did not simply create the world and then walk away to let it run on its own. He is intimately involved in every detail of His creation. This ongoing care and direction of the world is what we call "providence."

This chapter explores how God's providence works in our daily lives. We will see that God is the one who provides our needs, protects us from harm, and directs our steps according to His wise plan. When we trust in God's providence, we can trade our anxiety for peace, knowing that the One who rules the stars also cares for the smallest details of our day.

What is Providence?

The word "providence" comes from the Latin *providere*, which means "to see ahead" or "to provide." It refers to God's continued exercise of the same power by which He created all things, now used to sustain them and direct them to their intended end.

Scripture teaches that God is not a distant observer. He is the one who "upholds the universe by the word of his power" (Hebrews 1:3). Providence means that there is no such thing as "luck," "fate," or "accidents" in a world ruled by a sovereign God. Everything that happens, from the spinning of a galaxy to the landing of a sparrow, is under His watchful eye and governed by His hand.

God Sustains All Things

The first aspect of providence is preservation. God keeps all things in existence. If God were to withdraw His hand for a single moment, the entire universe would cease to exist.

The Bible tells us that in God's hand "is the life of every living thing and the breath of all mankind" (Job 12:10). We see this in the regular patterns of nature, the rising of the sun, the changing of seasons, and the growth of crops. When we wake up each morning, we are experiencing the sustaining providence of God. He provides the air we breathe and the heartbeat that keeps us alive.

God Governs Every Detail

The second aspect of providence is government. God directs all things to fulfill His purposes. This includes the natural world, the affairs of nations, and the individual lives of people.

- **Nature:** God commands the clouds, the wind, and the rain (Psalm 147:8).

- **Nations:** He raises up kings and removes them; He sets the boundaries of people (Daniel 2:21; Acts 17:26).

- **Individuals:** Our days are written in His book before we are even born (Psalm 139:16).

Even the "random" events of life are under His control. Proverbs 16:33 says, "The lot is cast into the lap, but its every decision is from the LORD." This doesn't mean we are robots; we make real choices and are responsible for them, but God is so great that He works through our choices to accomplish His perfect will.

The Purpose of Providence: Our Good and His Glory

Why does God exercise such detailed control? As we saw in Chapter 16, His ultimate goal is His own glory and the good of His people.

The most famous promise regarding providence is Romans 8:28: "And we know that for those who love God all things work together for good, for those who are called according to his purpose". This means that even when we face trials, delays, or disappointments, God is weaving those threads into a beautiful tapestry. He uses the difficult moments to shape our character, strengthen our faith, and lead us closer to Him.

Responding to Providence with Trust

Knowing that God is in control should change how we face each day. If a loving, wise, and powerful Father is directing our lives, then we have no reason to be paralyzed by worry.

Jesus used the doctrine of providence to attack anxiety. He pointed out that the Father feeds the birds and clothes the lilies—things that are much less valuable than we are (Matthew 6:25–34). If the Father takes care of them, we can trust Him to provide for us. Trusting in providence means learning to say, "The Lord will provide," even when we cannot see the solution yet.

Resting in God's Timing

Often, God's providence doesn't move as fast as we would like. We pray for a change, and the answer seems delayed. However, providence reminds us that God's timing is perfect because His wisdom is perfect.

Resting in providence means submitting our "to-do lists" and our "life plans" to Him. It means being content with where He has placed us today, knowing that we are exactly where we need to be for His current work in our lives.

Weekly Belief Statement

We believe that God, in His infinite power and wisdom, sustains and governs all creatures and all events, from the greatest to the least. We believe that His providence is always directed toward His own glory and the good of His people. We trust that nothing happens by chance, but everything comes to us from His fatherly hand.

Practical Application

✝ **Audit Your Worries:** Make a list of three things you are currently anxious about. Next to each one, write: "God is sovereign over this, and He is my Provider".

✝ **Find God in the Details:** At the end of each day this week, look back and identify one "small" thing that went well (a green light when you were late, a kind word from a stranger, an unexpected check). Thank God for His specific providence in that moment.

✝ **Pray Over Your Plans:** Before you start your workday or a big project, pray: "Lord, these are my plans, but I submit them to Your providence. Direct my steps today".

✝ **Read the Story of Joseph:** Read Genesis 50:15–21. Reflect on how God used even the evil actions of others to bring about a providential "good".

✝ **Practice Contentment:** When you face a frustration or a delay this week, stop and remind yourself: "God has a purpose for this moment. I will trust His timing".

"The LORD has established his throne in the heavens, and his kingdom rules over all". - Psalm 103:19

CHAPTER 20
Recognize God's Special Acts in History

In our previous study of providence, we marveled at how God constantly sustains and governs the ordinary operations of the world, the "laws of nature" that keep the stars in their courses and the seasons in their cycle. However, the Bible reveals that God is not a distant clockmaker who simply lets the world run on its own. Throughout history, He has stepped into time and space in extraordinary ways to accomplish His specific purposes. These "special acts" remind us that God is a personal, active King who is deeply involved in the human story.

This chapter explores how we recognize these unique interventions. We will look at the nature of miracles, the distinction between general and special revelation, and the ultimate "special act" that split history in two. When we recognize God's special acts, we find a faith that is not based on abstract ideas, but on real events that actually happened.

Defining Special Acts: Beyond the Ordinary

To understand special acts, we must first understand the "ordinary" way God works. In Chapter 19, we saw that God is the primary cause of everything—He is the one who makes the grass grow and the rain fall. We call this "General Providence." However, "Special Acts" occur when God works without, above, or against the ordinary means of nature to reveal His power and plan.

Special acts serve as "signs". They are not just random displays of power; they point toward a greater truth. In the Bible, God uses these moments to authenticate His messengers, deliver His people, or fulfill a specific promise. Recognizing these acts helps us see that the God of the Bible is a "Living God" who speaks and acts in real-time.

The Theology of Miracles

The most prominent special acts in Scripture are miracles. A miracle is an event in the external world, wrought by the immediate efficiency of God, intended to be a sign.

Miracles in Scripture are rarely "parlor tricks" to entertain. They usually appear in "clusters" around major turning points in redemptive history. We see them most frequently during the Exodus from Egypt, the ministries of Elijah and Elisha, and the ministry of Jesus and the Apostles. Their purpose is multi-fold:

1. **To Authenticate the Messenger:** When God sends a prophet with a new message, He often grants them the power to perform miracles to prove they are truly speaking for Him.

2. **To Demonstrate Divine Authority:** Miracles show that God is not a prisoner of His own laws. He has total authority over nature (calming the storm), disease (healing the leper), and even death (raising Lazarus).

3. **To Effect Deliverance:** Many special acts are acts of rescue. God parts the Red Sea not just to show off, but to save His people from an impossible situation.

Special Acts of Revelation

God also acts specially by revealing specific information that nature alone cannot communicate. While "General Revelation" tells us God is powerful and wise through the things He has made, it does not tell us His name, His moral laws, or His plan for salvation.

God's special acts of revelation include:

✝ **The Establishment of Covenants:** These are specific, formal agreements God initiated with people like Noah, Abraham, Moses, and David to unfold His plan of redemption.

✝ **The Inspiration of Scripture:** The act of the Holy Spirit guiding human authors to record God's truth without error is a massive "special act" that spans centuries.

✝ **Prophetic Foretelling:** By predicting future events with 100% accuracy, God proves He alone is the Lord of history who knows and ordains the end from the beginning.

The Climax of History: The Incarnation and Resurrection

The greatest special act in all of history—the act that all previous chapters of this book have pointed toward—is the Incarnation. This is the moment when the eternal Son of God, the second Person of the Trinity, took on human flesh and dwelt among us. This was not a natural development of evolution; it was a miraculous intervention that forever changed the relationship between God and humanity.

Following the Incarnation is the special act of the Resurrection. The physical rising of Jesus from the dead is the supreme miracle of the Christian faith. If Jesus did not rise, our faith is in vain. But because He did, the Resurrection stands as the ultimate "sign" that God has conquered sin and death and is making all things new.

Understanding the "Shape" of History

Recognizing God's special acts helps us understand that history is not a series of random accidents or a circular loop. History has a "shape" and a destination. It is a story directed by a Sovereign King moving toward a specific climax.

God acts in history to bring about the "fullness of time." He spent centuries preparing the world for the first coming of Christ—through the law, the prophets, and the history of Israel. In the same way, He is currently governing history to prepare for Christ's return, when the final special acts of judgment and new creation will take place.

Responding to God's Acts Today

While we live in an age where we might not see the Red Sea part every day, we are called to be a people who "Recognize" and "Remember" these acts:

1. **Trust the Written Record:** We do not need to witness a miracle ourselves to be certain of it. We have the reliable, God-breathed record of Scripture that testifies to these events.

2. **Recount His Deeds in Worship:** Much of the Bible's poetry and song is simply a retelling of God's special acts. When we worship, we are reminding ourselves of what our God has actually done in history.

3. **Live with "Supernatural" Expectation:** Recognizing special acts prevents us from becoming "practical deists"—people who believe in God but live as if He never interferes. We should pray with the confidence that God is still the Living Lord who can act in "extraordinary" ways according to His will.

Conclusion: The Anchor of Our Hope

If God never acted specially, we would be a people without hope, trapped in a closed system of cause and effect. But because God has stepped into history, most clearly in the person of Jesus Christ, we know that the "impossible" is God's specialty. Recognizing His special acts in the past gives us the courage to trust His promises for the future.

Weekly Belief Statement

We believe that God is the Living Lord who acts specially in history to reveal His glory and accomplish His salvation. We affirm that miracles are real, historical signs of His authority over all creation. We believe He has specially revealed His character and will through the Covenants, the Holy Scriptures, and ultimately through the Incarnation of His Son, Jesus Christ. We believe that history is not a series of accidents but a purposeful story directed by God toward its promised fulfillment.

Practical Application

- **Identify the Landmarks:** Spend time this week reading through the "Hall of Faith" in Hebrews 11. List the special acts mentioned and what each one revealed about God's character.

- **Trace the Trinity:** Look at the major special acts (Creation, the Exodus, the Incarnation, the Resurrection). How do you see the Father, Son, and Spirit working together in these historical moments?

- **Combat Small-Mindedness:** When you face a "mountain" in your life this week, stop and remind yourself of the God who parted the sea. Ask yourself: "Is my problem bigger than the God of history?"

- **Read the "Acts of God":** Read Psalm 77. Notice how the psalmist overcomes his distress by intentionally "remembering the deeds of the LORD" and "your wonders of old."

- **Share the Story:** Choose one historical act of God (like the Resurrection or a time He clearly intervened in your own life) and tell someone about it this week as a way of testifying to His living power.

"He is the LORD our God; his judgments are in all the earth. He remembers his covenant forever, the word that he commanded, for a thousand generations." Psalm 105:7–8

CHAPTER 21
Hold On to God's Goodness in Suffering

Perhaps the greatest challenge to any theological system is the reality of pain. When a child falls ill, a natural disaster strikes, or a life is marked by chronic disappointment, the truths we have studied, God's power, His plan, and His providence, can feel like they are being put on trial. We find ourselves asking the hard questions that have echoed through the centuries: If God is all-powerful and perfectly good, why is there so much suffering?.

This chapter does not offer a simple "fix" for pain, but it provides a biblical framework for enduring it. We will see that while suffering is a result of a broken world, it is never outside of God's control or beyond His ability to use for good. When we hold on to God's goodness in the dark, our faith moves from a theoretical idea to an unshakeable anchor.

The Origin of Suffering: A Broken World

To understand suffering, we must look back to the Fall. Suffering was not part of God's "very good" original creation. It entered the world through human rebellion, a topic we will address in depth in Part 5. Because of sin, the world is now "subjected to futility".

Disease, decay, and death are intruders in God's world. This means that much of the suffering we experience is not a sign that God is angry with us personally, but a sign that we live in a world that is waiting to be made new. Recognizing this prevents us from blaming God's character for the consequences of sin's entry into the world.

God Is Sovereign Over Suffering

One of the most comforting, yet difficult, truths is that God remains sovereign even over our pain. He is not a helpless bystander watching tragedy unfold. The Bible teaches that God sits on His throne even when the waters roar and foam.

Consider the life of Job. He lost his wealth, his children, and his health in a single season. Yet, at the end of his ordeal, God did not apologize for being absent; He reminded Job of His immense power and wisdom. God is so great that He can fold even the most painful events into His eternal plan without ever becoming the author of evil Himself. As Joseph famously told his brothers who had sold him into slavery: "As for you, you meant evil against me, but God meant it for good."

The Purpose in the Pain

While we rarely know the specific reason for a particular trial, Scripture gives us several general purposes for why God allows His children to suffer:

- **To Refine Our Faith:** Just as gold is purified in the fire, our faith is often strengthened through the "heat" of trials.

- **To Draw Us Nearer to Him:** In times of ease, we often forget our need for God. In suffering, we find that the Lord is near to the brokenhearted.

- **To Produce Character:** Scripture teaches that suffering produces endurance, endurance produces character, and character produces hope.

- **To Comfort Others:** When we experience God's comfort in our pain, we become equipped to comfort others who face similar trials.

The Compassion of the Suffering Savior

The Christian response to suffering is unique because our God did not remain distant from it. In the person of Jesus Christ, God entered into human suffering. He is described as a "man of sorrows and acquainted with grief".

When you suffer, you are not crying out to a God who doesn't understand. You are crying out to a Savior who felt physical pain, the sting of betrayal, the weight of loneliness, and the agony of death. Because Jesus suffered for us, our own suffering is no longer a sign of God's rejection. Instead, it becomes a way we share in His journey as we wait for His glory.

Lament: Giving Voice to the Pain

God does not ask us to pretend that pain doesn't hurt. The Bible is full of "lament"—honest, raw cries to God in the midst of distress. Over a third of the Psalms are psalms of lament, asking "How long, O Lord?" or "Why have you forsaken me?".

Lament is not the same as grumbling. Grumbling is complaining *about* God; lament is complaining *to* God. It is an act of faith because it brings the pain to the only One who can actually help. God is big enough to handle your honest questions and your deepest tears.

The Hope of Future Glory

Finally, we hold on to goodness by looking at the "End" of our map: hope. The current suffering, no matter how heavy, is not the end of the story. Paul, who faced beatings and imprisonment, called his trials a "light momentary affliction" compared to the "eternal weight of glory" that was coming.

One day, God will wipe away every tear, and death, mourning, and pain shall be no more. Our hope is not just that the pain will stop, but that God will eventually make "all things new". The goodness of God is the guarantee that the story ends in a New Creation where suffering is forgotten in the light of His presence.

Weekly Belief Statement

We believe that suffering entered the world through sin but remains under the sovereign hand of a good and wise God. We believe that God uses trials to refine our faith, grow our character, and draw us closer to Himself. We affirm that Jesus Christ is our compassionate Savior who suffered on our behalf, and we rest in the certain hope that He will one day end all suffering in the New Creation.

Practical Application

- **Practice Lament:** If you are in a season of pain, read a psalm of lament. Use its structure to talk to God: complain honestly about your trouble, ask for His help, and then choose to trust in His steadfast love.

- **Look for the "But God":** Reflect on a past trial. Can you see a moment where you could say, "This was meant for evil, *but God* used it for good"?. Write that down as a reminder for the future.

- **Identify a Purpose:** If you are currently struggling, ask God: "Lord, what are You teaching me right now? How can this trial make me more like Jesus?".

- **Be a Comfort to Others:** Look for someone in your church or community who is suffering. Don't feel the need to give them "answers"; simply offer the same comfort God has given you in the past.

✝ **Memorize the End of the Story:** Commit a verse about the New Creation to memory this week. When you feel overwhelmed by the brokenness of the world, recite it to remind your soul of where history is heading.

"For I consider that the sufferings of this present time are not worth comparing with the glory that is to be revealed to us." - Romans 8:18

CHAPTER 22
Honor People as God's Image-Bearers

If you walk into a great art gallery, you might see a painting that looks like a few random splashes of color. To an untrained eye, it might seem worthless. But if the gallery owner tells you that it was painted by a world-renowned master, your perspective shifts instantly. You wouldn't dare touch it or deface it; you would treat it with a specific kind of reverence because of who created it.

The Bible makes a startling claim about every human being you will ever meet: they are a masterpiece. In the opening chapter of Genesis, after God created the stars, the seas, and the animals, He did something unique. He created humanity "in his own image" (Genesis 1:26-27). This is the doctrine of the *Imago Dei*. It is the foundation of human dignity, the basis for human rights, and the reason why how we treat one another is a direct reflection of how we feel about God.

What Does It Mean to Be the "Image of God"?

For centuries, theologians have debated exactly what this "image" entails. Is it our ability to think? Our creativity? Our capacity for relationship? While it likely includes all those things, the most important part is that it is a *status*. To be an image-bearer means that humans are created to be God's representatives on earth. Just as an ancient king would set up a statue (an image) of himself in a distant part of his kingdom to show who was in charge, God placed us in His world to reflect His character and carry out His work.

This image was not "lost" during the Fall, though it was certainly "marred" or "cracked." Like a mirror that has been dropped, every person still reflects God, but the reflection is distorted by sin. Yet, even in this broken state, the image remains. This is why, later in the Bible, God tells Noah that murder is a capital offense—not just because it ends a life, but because to kill a human is to strike at the image of God (Genesis 9:6).

The Source of Inherent Dignity

In our modern world, we often assign value to people based on what they can *do*. We value the productive, the brilliant, the beautiful, and the strong. By default, this implies that the weak, the unborn, the elderly, or those with disabilities have less value.

The doctrine of the *Imago Dei* flips this entirely. Human dignity is not something we earn through performance; it is something we possess by birth. Dignity is "inherent"—it is woven into our very DNA by the Creator.

✝ **The Unborn:** Value is present from conception because God is the one "knitting" the image together in the womb.

✝ **The Elderly:** Value does not decrease as productivity fades; the image remains as vibrant in a nursing home as it does in a boardroom.

✝ **The Marginalized:** No matter a person's social status, wealth, or background, they bear the royal likeness of the King of the universe.

The Image and Our Relationships

If we truly believe that every person is an image-bearer, it changes the way we talk, act, and think about others. The Apostle James makes a stinging observation about the tongue: "With it we bless our Lord and Father, and with it we curse people who are made in the likeness of God... these things ought not to be so" (James 3:9–10).

We cannot claim to love God while despising His image in our neighbor. This means that racism, sexism, and classism are not just social problems; they are theological errors. They are a denial of the *Imago Dei*. When we look at someone who looks different, speaks a different language, or holds a different political view, our first thought should not be "them," but "image-bearer."

The Restoration of the Image in Christ

While we all bear the image of God by creation, we see the *perfect* image of God in only one person: Jesus Christ. Colossians 1:15 says, "He is the image of the invisible God." Jesus shows us what humanity was actually supposed to look like. He was perfectly dependent on the Father, perfectly loving toward others, and perfectly holy in His character.

The "good news" of the gospel is that God is in the business of restoring His image in us. Through the work of the Holy Spirit, we are being "conformed to the image of his Son" (Romans 8:29). When we follow Jesus, we are not becoming less human; we are becoming *more* human. We are returning to the original design God intended in the Garden.

Honoring the Image in Ourselves

Sometimes the hardest person to honor as an image-bearer is yourself. Many of us struggle with deep feelings of worthlessness, shame, or self-hatred. We look in the mirror and see only the "cracks" and none of the "image."

But the doctrine of the *Imago Dei* tells you that you are not a mistake. Your life has objective meaning because God decided to put His likeness on you. Your value is not determined by your past mistakes, your current struggles, or the opinions of others. You belong to Him. Honoring the image means taking care of your body, stewardng your mind, and refusing to believe the lie that your life doesn't matter.

Stewardship: The Task of the Image-Bearer

Finally, being an image-bearer involves a task. As we saw in Chapter 18, God gave humanity "dominion" over the earth. This isn't a license to destroy or exploit; it is a call to represent God's wise and loving rule. We are called to be gardeners, creators, and protectors.

When we work, when we create art, when we raise children, and when we seek justice, we are acting out our identity as image-bearers. We are showing the world what God is like. Our goal is to make the invisible God visible through our visible lives.

Weekly Belief Statement

We believe that every human being, from conception to natural death, is created in the image of God and possesses inherent dignity, value, and worth. We believe that this image, though marred by sin, remains the foundation for how we must treat one another. We affirm that Jesus Christ is the perfect image of God and that, through Him, we are being restored to our original purpose.

Practical Application

✝ **The "Image-Bearer" Filter:** This week, before you post a comment online or speak about someone behind their back, stop and say: "That person is an image-bearer of God." Notice how this changes your words.

✝ **Affirm Value:** Find someone in your life who feels overlooked or marginalized (perhaps a service worker, a lonely neighbor, or a difficult coworker). Intentionally look them in the eye and treat them with "royal" dignity.

✝ **Steward Your Talents:** Think of one skill or creative outlet you have. How can you use that today to reflect God's creativity to those around you?

✝ **Read the Creation Account:** Read Genesis 1:26–31 again. Pay attention to the "deliberation" God has before creating humans. Reflect on the fact that you were made with intentionality.

✝ **Combat Self-Hatred:** If you find yourself thinking "I am worthless" this week, counter that thought with the truth: "I am an image-bearer of the King, and He does not make junk."

"So God created man in his own image, in the image of God he created him; male and female he created them." -
Genesis 1:27

CHAPTER 23
Live Out God's Good Design for Men and Women

In the previous chapter, we established that every human being bears the royal image of God. But the Bible doesn't stop with our shared humanity. It immediately highlights a specific, beautiful distinction: "male and female he created them" (Genesis 1:27). Our sex is not an accident of nature or a social construct we invent for ourselves; it is a fundamental part of God's "very good" design.

This chapter explores what it means to live out this design. We will see that men and women are created with absolute equality in value, yet with a purposeful distinction in how they reflect God's glory. When we embrace God's design for the sexes, we find a harmony that honors the Creator and helps society flourish.

Equality in Being

The starting point for any Christian discussion on men and women must be their total equality. Both men and women are created in the image of God. Both are given the mandate to rule over the earth. Both are fallen in sin, and both are redeemed by the same grace through faith in Christ.

In the kingdom of God, there is no "first-class" or "second-class" citizen based on sex. As Paul wrote to the Galatians, "there is no male and female, for you are all one in Christ Jesus" (Galatians 3:28). This means that a woman's soul is not "lesser" than a man's, nor is a man's voice "more important" to God than a woman's. Any system or attitude that treats one sex as inherently superior to the other is a violation of the creation order.

Distinction in Design

Equality, however, does not mean "sameness." Throughout the Bible, we see that God delights in diversity. Just as the three Persons of the

Trinity are equal in essence but distinct in their roles, men and women reflect different aspects of God's character.

Maleness and femaleness are biological and spiritual realities that run deep into who we are. From the beginning, God described the woman as a "helper" for the man (Genesis 2:18). In modern ears, "helper" can sound like a demeaning term, but in the Bible, the word *ezer* is most often used to describe God Himself as He helps His people. It implies a "necessary ally"—someone who brings strengths to the table that the other lacks. Men and women are like two different movements in a single symphony; they are different, but they are designed to play together.

The Beauty of Complementarity

The term often used for this is "complementarianism." It is the idea that men and women complement, or complete, one another. Where one is strong, the other may be soft; where one provides, the other may nurture.

This design is most clearly seen in the covenant of marriage. God designed marriage to be a living picture of the relationship between Christ and the Church (Ephesians 5:22–33). In this picture:

✝ **Men** are called to a specific kind of sacrificial leadership, modeled after Christ who gave His life for His bride.

✝ **Women** are called to a specific kind of supportive partnership, modeled after the Church that honors and follows Christ.

When men lead with humility and women partner with strength, the world gets a glimpse of the gospel.

Beyond the Home

God's design for men and women isn't just about marriage; it affects how we interact as a human family. Men are generally called to a "fatherly" strength, a protective, providing, and initiating presence. Women are generally called to a "motherly" wisdom, a nurturing, life-giving, and discerning presence.

A world without distinct masculinity is a world that lacks protection and structure; a world without distinct femininity is a world that lacks warmth and beauty. We need both. We should celebrate the man who uses his strength to serve others, and we should honor the woman who uses her influence to cultivate life and truth.

The Friction of the Fall

We must be honest: this is an area where we feel the most "friction" today. Because of the Fall, the relationship between the sexes has been broken. Throughout history, men have often used their strength to dominate or abuse, and women have often faced oppression or responded with manipulation.

The "battle of the sexes" is a result of sin. But in Christ, we are called to a new way of living. We don't have to follow the toxic stereotypes of the world. Men don't have to be aggressive or silent; they can be "gentle giants" like Jesus. Women don't have to be hidden or harsh; they can be "valiant warriors" for the truth.

Honoring the Body

Living out God's design also means accepting the body God gave us. In a culture that often suggests our "true self" is something separate from our physical sex, the Bible calls us back to the goodness of the body. Your biological sex is a gift from God. To be a man is a calling; to be a woman is a calling.

We honor God when we live in accordance with the sex He assigned to us, rather than trying to rewrite the "very good" script He wrote for our lives. This requires humility, but it leads to the peace of living as who we truly are.

Weekly Belief Statement

We believe that God created humanity as male and female, and that this distinction is a fundamental part of His good design. We affirm the total equality of men and women in dignity and value, while recognizing their distinct and complementary roles in the home, the church, and society. We believe that embracing our biological sex as a gift from God leads to human flourishing and reflects the glory of the Creator.

Practical Application

- **Celebrate the Other:** This week, take a moment to thank God specifically for the strengths of the opposite sex. If you are a man, thank God for the women in your life; if you are a woman, thank God for the men.

- **Reject Stereotypes, Embrace Design:** Look at your own life. Are you following a cultural stereotype (like "men shouldn't show emotion") or a biblical design (like "men should be sacrificial")? Choose one biblical quality of your sex to lean into this week.

✝ **Pray for Your Relationships:** If there is tension between you and someone of the opposite sex, ask the Spirit to help you see them as an equal image-bearer with a distinct design.

✝ **Read the Pattern:** Read Proverbs 31 (for women) or 1 Timothy 3:1-7 (for men). Don't see these as impossible lists, but as beautiful "target" character traits for your life.

✝ **Encourage a Younger Person:** Find a young man or woman in your circle and encourage them in their specific identity. Tell a boy, "I love the way you use your strength to help," or tell a girl, "I love the wisdom and care you show to others."

"So God created man in his own image, in the image of God he created him; male and female he created them." -
Genesis 1:27

CHAPTER 24
Obey God's Moral Law With Faith

In the modern world, the word "law" often feels restrictive. We think of speed limits, taxes, or "do not enter" signs. We tend to view laws as barriers to our freedom. But in the Bible, God's law is described as a gift. It is like a manual for a complex machine; it tells us how we were designed to function so that we don't break ourselves.

This chapter explores God's moral law, the timeless standards of right and wrong that reflect His holy character. We will see that we don't obey the law to *earn* God's love, but because we *already have* His love. When we obey with faith, we find that God's commands are not a burden, but the pathway to true life.

The Nature of God's Moral Law

The moral law is not a set of arbitrary rules God made up on a whim. Because God is the Creator, His law is a reflection of His own nature. Since God is truthful, He commands us not to lie. Since God is faithful, He commands us to be faithful.

The most famous summary of this law is the **Ten Commandments** (Exodus 20). These are divided into two parts: our duty toward God and our duty toward our neighbor. Jesus later summarized these even further: "Love the Lord your God with all your heart... and love your neighbor as yourself" (Matthew 22:37-40). The law is essentially a description of what perfect love looks like in action.

The Three Purposes of the Law

If we cannot be saved by keeping the law (because we all fail to keep it perfectly), why did God give it to us? Traditionally, Christians have recognized three "uses" for the law:

1. **A Mirror:** The law shows us God's perfect standard and, in doing so, reveals our own sin. Like a mirror, it doesn't wash our face, but it shows us that we are dirty and need the "water" of God's grace. It drives us to Christ.

2. **A Restraint:** The law provides a moral boundary for society. Even for those who don't follow God, the presence of moral standards helps prevent the world from falling into total chaos.

3. **A Guide:** For the believer, the law is a "lamp to our feet." It shows us how to live a life that pleases the Father. It is the "rule of gratitude" for the Christian life.

Obedience Is the Fruit of Faith

A common mistake is to think that faith and obedience are opposites. Some people think, "If I have faith, I don't need to worry about the law." But true faith always produces obedience.

Think of a fruit tree. The roots (faith) are hidden underground, but the fruit (obedience) is what everyone sees. If there is no fruit, the roots are likely dead. We are saved by faith *alone,* but the faith that saves is never *alone.* It always brings a desire to honor God's commands. When we obey, we aren't trying to get God to notice us; we are showing that we have noticed Him.

The Law Written on the Heart

Under the "New Covenant," God promised something incredible: "I will put my law within them, and I will write it on their hearts" (Jeremiah 31:33).

In the Old Testament, the law was on tablets of stone—outside the person. In Christ, through the Holy Spirit, the law is moved inside the person. This means that for the Christian, obedience isn't just a "duty" we force ourselves to do. It becomes a "delight." We begin to want what God wants. We don't just avoid stealing because we fear the police; we avoid it because we love our neighbor and want to honor God.

Living Under Grace, Not Legalism

We must be careful to avoid "legalism." Legalism is the belief that our standing with God depends on our performance. It turns the Christian life into a scorecard.

If you obey God's law to feel superior to others, or to try and put God in your debt, you are practicing legalism. But the gospel tells us that our "score" was settled by Jesus. He kept the law perfectly for us. Now, we obey from a position of security, not from a position of fear. We are like children who want to make their Father proud, not like slaves who are afraid of being whipped.

The Freedom of Boundaries

True freedom is not the ability to do whatever you want; it is the ability to do what you were made for. A fish is "free" only when it stays within the "boundary" of the water. If it tries to be "free" on the grass, it dies.

In the same way, God's moral law provides the environment where human life flourishes. When we follow His design for sex, for honesty, for rest (the Sabbath), and for worship, we find that our lives "work" better. The world tells us that boundaries are oppressive, but the believer knows that God's boundaries are protective.

Weekly Belief Statement

We believe that God's moral law is a holy and perfect reflection of His character. We affirm that while no one can be saved by keeping the law, it remains a vital guide for the Christian life. We believe that true faith naturally produces a desire to obey God's commands out of gratitude for His grace, and we look to the Holy Spirit to empower us to live in accordance with His Word.

Practical Application

- **Examine the Mirror:** Read the Ten Commandments in Exodus 20. Instead of looking for where you "succeeded," ask the Spirit to show you one area where you have fallen short. Take that specific sin to Jesus for forgiveness.

- **Choose Delight Over Duty:** Identify one command you find difficult (like "do not grumble" or "forgive others"). This week, try to obey it not as a "have to," but as a "get to", an opportunity to show God you love Him.

- **Audit Your Motives:** Ask yourself: "When I do something good, am I doing it so people think I'm holy, or because I'm thankful to God?" Repent of any legalism you find.

- **Read the Praise of the Law:** Read Psalm 119:97–104. Notice how the author uses words like "sweet" and "honey" to describe God's rules. Pray for a heart that loves God's Word that much.

- **The "Love Test":** When you are faced with a moral choice this week, ask: "How does the law of love apply here? How can I honor God and help my neighbor in this moment?"

"If you love me, you will keep my commandments." - John 14:15

PART FIVE
Face Sin and God's Justice

CHAPTER 25
Name Sin Honestly

In the previous chapters, we have stood on the mountain peaks of theology. We have marveled at the glory of the Trinity, the majesty of creation, and the dignity of being made in God's image. But to understand the story of the world—and the story of our own lives—we must eventually descend into the valley. We have to talk about the one thing that explains why a world so beautiful is also so broken. We have to talk about sin.

In our modern world, "sin" has become a word people use for jokes or for food that has too many calories. We prefer to speak of "mistakes," "issues," "maladjustments," or "miscalculations." We use clinical language to soften the blow. But if we are to find a real cure, we must be honest about the disease. This chapter is about calling sin by its real name. We will see that sin is not just "breaking a rule"; it is a rebellion against a person, a rejection of our design, and a spiritual suicide. When we name sin honestly, we are finally ready to appreciate the magnitude of God's grace.

Sin Is More Than an Error

The first step in naming sin honestly is realizing that it is not merely a mistake. A mistake is forgetting your keys or getting a math problem wrong. Sin is something deeper. The primary words for sin in the Bible describe it in three ways:

✝ **Missing the Mark:** This is the most common term. It describes an archer who aims for a target but falls short. God's "mark" is His perfect holiness. When we sin, we fail to meet the standard of why we were created.

✝ **Transgression:** This means "stepping over a line." God has set moral boundaries for our protection. When we sin, we see the boundary and choose to cross it anyway.

✝ **Iniquity:** This refers to "crookedness" or "perversion." It is the idea of something that was meant to be straight and beautiful being twisted and warped.

Sin is a "vandalism of shalom." God created a world of peace, order, and harmony (shalom). Sin is the active tearing down of that harmony. It is the act of taking God's good gifts and using them for our own selfish ends.

Sin Is Relational Rebellion

We often think of sin as a violation of a law, but the Bible frames it as a violation of a relationship. Because God is our Father, Creator, and King, our sin is a personal offense against Him. When King David committed adultery and murder, he later prayed, "Against you, you only, have I sinned and done what is evil in your sight" (Psalm 51:4). David knew he had hurt people, but he realized the deepest sting of his sin was that he had betrayed the God who loved him.

Think of sin as "cosmic treason." It is the creature telling the Creator, "I don't need You. I want to be my own god. I want to define my own truth." Every sin, no matter how small it seems to us, is a vote for our own independence from the Source of Life. This is why sin is so serious. It isn't just a "slip-up"; it is a declaration of war against the most loving Being in the universe.

The Anatomy of a Lie

How does sin work? It always begins with a lie. In the Garden of Eden, the serpent didn't start by telling Eve to kill someone. He started by questioning God's Word: "Did God actually say...?" and then questioning God's character: "You will not surely die... God knows that when you eat of it your eyes will be opened."

The lie at the heart of every sin is that God is holding out on us. We believe that His commands are meant to keep us from happiness, and that we know better than He does what will satisfy us. We think that by stepping outside of His will, we will find "real" freedom. But as we soon discover, the freedom to sin is actually the freedom to be a slave to our own desires.

Sin as Internal, Not Just External

A common mistake is thinking that sin is only what we *do*: he big, visible actions like stealing or lying. But Jesus taught that sin begins in the heart. He said that anger is the seed of murder and lust is the seed of adultery (Matthew 5:21–28).

Sin is a heart condition. It is a "disordered love." We were made to love God first and others second. Sin flips that upside down. We love ourselves first, our comfort second, and God somewhere down at the bottom of the list. Even our "good" deeds can be sinful if they are done for the wrong reasons, like trying to look holy or trying to manipulate God into giving us what we want.

The Deceptive Nature of Sin

One of the most dangerous things about sin is that it never presents itself as "evil" at the beginning. It always promises a reward. It offers a shortcut to pleasure, power, or security.

Hebrews 3:13 warns us about the "deceitfulness of sin." Sin hardens the heart slowly. Like a frog in a pot of water that is slowly coming to a boil, we get used to "small" compromises until our conscience is seared. We start by excusing a little bit of gossip, then a little bit of dishonesty, and before we know it, our spiritual life is in ruins. Naming sin honestly means seeing the "hook" behind the "bait."

Sin as a Power and a Debt

The Bible describes sin in two legal and spiritual ways that help us understand our need for a Savior.

1. **Sin as a Debt:** Every time we rebel against God's law, we incur a moral debt. We owe God a perfect life of obedience that we cannot pay. We are "bankrupt" before the court of heaven. This is why we need a substitute to pay our debt.

2. **Sin as a Power:** Sin is also a force that grips us. Jesus said, "Everyone who practices sin is a slave to sin" (John 8:34). It's not just that we *have* sinned; it's that we *can't stop* sinning on our own. We are trapped in a cycle of habits and desires that we cannot break by willpower alone.

Total Depravity: A Human Condition

When theologians speak of "Total Depravity," they don't mean that every human is as evil as they could possibly be. It means that sin has affected every *part* of us: our minds, our emotions, our bodies, and our wills. There is no "clean" corner of the human heart.

Even our best moments are tainted with a little bit of pride or selfishness. This is a hard truth to swallow because we like to think of ourselves as "basically good people." But naming sin honestly means admitting that the line between good and evil doesn't run between "us" and "them"; it runs right through the middle of every human heart.

Why Naming Sin Is Good News

Talking about sin feels heavy, but it is actually the doorway to joy. You cannot appreciate the "Good News" of the gospel until you hear the "Bad News" of your condition.

If you are sick but refuse to admit it, you will never go to the doctor. If you are drowning but refuse to admit you can't swim, you will never reach for the life ring. Naming sin honestly is the first step of repentance. It is the moment the Prodigal Son "came to himself" and realized he was eating pig food while his Father had a feast waiting. When we stop making excuses and say, "Lord, have mercy on me, a sinner," we find that God is more ready to forgive than we are to ask.

Weekly Belief Statement

We believe that sin is a universal human reality, a personal rebellion against the holy and loving God. We affirm that sin is not merely a mistake, but a rejection of our Creator's design that has corrupted every part of our being. We confess that we are guilty of sin in our thoughts, words, and deeds, and that we are powerless to save ourselves from the debt and power of sin apart from God's grace.

Practical Application

- **Drop the Euphemisms:** This week, when you fail, don't say "I had a lapse in judgment" or "I was just tired." Try saying, "I sinned against God by being [angry/dishonest/selfish]." Notice how "owning" the word changes your heart.

- **Search the Heart:** Spend ten minutes in silence. Ask the Holy Spirit to show you a "hidden" sin, perhaps a grudge you are holding or a subtle pride. Don't hide from it; bring it into the light.

- **Read the Great Confession:** Read Psalm 51 slowly. Pay attention to how David describes his sin and what he asks God to do about it. Make his words your own.

- **Identify the Lie:** Think of a temptation you struggle with. What is the "lie" behind it? What is it promising you that only God can truly provide?

- **Practice "Immediate Repentance":** The moment you realize you have sinned this week, stop and confess it immediately to God. Don't wait until the end of the day. Keep "short accounts" with your Father.

"If we say we have no sin, we deceive ourselves, and the truth is not in us. If we confess our sins, he is faithful and just to forgive us our sins and to cleanse us from all unrighteousness." - 1 John 1:8-9.

CHAPTER 26
Admit How the Fall Broke the World

If you have ever looked at a sunset and felt a deep sense of peace, only to turn on the news and see reports of war, famine, and injustice, you have experienced the great tension of human existence. We live in a world that is clearly beautiful, but just as clearly broken. There is a "wrongness" to life that we all feel, a sense that things aren't supposed to be this way.

In the previous chapter, we named the personal reality of sin. In this chapter, we widen our lens to see the cosmic consequences of the Fall. When the first humans rebelled against God, it wasn't just their souls that were affected; the entire "very good" creation was fractured. To admit how the Fall broke the world is to stop living in denial and to start longing for the only One who can put the pieces back together.

The Shattered Mirror: Broken Relationships

The first and most immediate effect of the Fall was the breaking of relationships. Before sin, Adam and Eve were "naked and unashamed," living in perfect transparency with God and each other. The moment they sinned, that harmony vanished.

- **The Break with God:** They hid. The God who was once their greatest joy became their greatest fear. Sin creates a barrier of shame and guilt that makes us want to run away from our Creator.

- **The Break with Each other:** Instead of protecting one another, they began to blame. Adam blamed Eve; Eve blamed the serpent. Every conflict, divorce, and war in history is an echo of this original fracture.

- **The Break with Self:** We now experience internal "disintegration." We feel shame, anxiety, and a lack of identity. We are at war with our own consciences.

The Groaning Creation: Natural Brokenness

One of the most sobering truths of Genesis 3 is that the physical earth was cursed because of human sin. God told Adam, "Cursed is the ground because of you; in pain you shall eat of it all the days of your life" (Genesis 3:17).

Nature, which was meant to be a garden of provision, became a wilderness of "thorns and thistles." This is why we face natural disasters, droughts, and the sheer difficulty of labor. The Apostle Paul describes this in Romans 8, saying that the "whole creation has been groaning together in the pains of childbirth until now." The world is literally "out of joint." When we see a hurricane or a cancer cell, we are seeing the physical ripples of a spiritual rebellion.

The Reign of Death

The ultimate "break" in the world is the introduction of death. God had warned that the penalty for rebellion would be death, and the Fall made that a reality. Death is the Great Interrupter. It is the final proof that the world is broken.

Death is both physical and spiritual. Physically, our bodies begin to decay the moment we are born. Spiritually, we are born separated from the source of life. The fact that we find death so unnatural, that we grieve and fight against it, is actually a proof that we were made for eternity. We hate death because it is an intruder that doesn't belong in God's original design.

Systematic Brokenness: The "Powers" at Work

Because the world is fallen, evil is not just individual; it is systematic. We live in a world where "the whole world lies in the power of the evil one" (1 John 5:19). This means that sin gets baked into our structures, our governments, our economies, and our cultures.

This is why even people with "good intentions" often end up participating in systems that hurt others. Injustice, poverty, and oppression are not just "accidents"; they are the results of a world that has turned away from its rightful King. To admit the world is broken is to realize that no human politician, technology, or education system can ever fully "fix" the problem. The rot is too deep.

The Futility of Life Without God

The Book of Ecclesiastes describes the fallen world as *hevel*, a Hebrew word meaning "vapor" or "breath." It often translates to "vanity" or "futility." In a broken world, we work hard only to have someone else enjoy the fruit of our labor. We build things that eventually crumble. We chase happiness only to find it slipping through our fingers.

Without God at the center, life in a fallen world feels like "chasing after the wind." This sense of futility is meant to be a mercy. It is designed to make us "homesick" for a world we have never seen but were made for. It forces us to stop looking to the creation for a satisfaction that only the Creator can give.

The Necessity of a New Creation

If the Fall broke the world so thoroughly, the solution cannot be a simple "patch job." We don't just need a little more morality or a better environment; we need a "New Creation."

Recognizing the depth of the break allows us to appreciate the depth of the rescue. God did not abandon the broken world. He promised that the "seed of the woman" would eventually crush the serpent's head. He promised that one day, the curse would be reversed. When we admit the world is broken, we are finally standing on the ground of reality, ready for the hope of the Gospel.

Weekly Belief Statement

We believe that the Fall of humanity resulted in a pervasive brokenness that affects every part of creation. We affirm that relationships are fractured, the physical world is subject to decay and disaster, and that death has entered human experience as the final consequence of sin. We confess that no human effort can repair this brokenness, and we look with hope toward God's promised renewal of all things.

Practical Application

- **Practice "Worldly Sorrow":** This week, when you see a news story about suffering or injustice, don't just scroll past. Stop and say, "Lord, the world is broken. Please come quickly." Let the brokenness fuel your prayers.

- **Identify the "Friction":** Where are you currently experiencing "thorns and thistles" in your work or home life? Instead of just being frustrated, acknowledge that this friction is a reminder that this world is not your final home.

- **Mend a Fracture:** Identify one relationship in your life that is currently "broken" or strained. Take a small step of humility or forgiveness this week to reflect the healing God wants to bring to a fallen world.

✝ **Read the "Groaning":** Read Romans 8:18-25. Pay attention to the hope that is offered even in the midst of the "groaning" of the world.

✝ **Look for the "Common Grace":** Even in a broken world, God is still kind. Find three things today that are still "very good" (a flower, a laugh, a meal) and thank God that His beauty still shines through the cracks.

"For the creation was subjected to futility, not willingly, but because of him who subjected it, in hope that the creation itself will be set free from its bondage to corruption." - Romans 8:20-21

CHAPTER 27
Fear God's Judgment and Seek His Mercy

In our journey through the "Map of Reality," we have reached a point that many people find deeply uncomfortable. We have talked about the beauty of God's design and the tragedy of our rebellion. Now, we must face the consequences. If God is the holy and just King of the universe, He cannot simply "look the other way" when His laws are broken and His image-bearers are harmed. Justice requires a reckoning.

This chapter explores the weight of God's judgment and the beauty of His mercy. In a culture that often views "fear" and "mercy" as opposites, the Bible presents them as two sides of the same coin. Without a proper fear of judgment, mercy seems cheap and unnecessary; without the hope of mercy, fear becomes a paralyzing despair. When we understand both, we find the only path to true peace.

The Necessity of Divine Judgment

We often struggle with the idea of a "God who judges." In our modern therapeutic age, we prefer to think of God only in terms of unconditional affirmation and soft kindness. But we must ask: would a God who *didn't* judge really be good?

Imagine a world where a judge ignores the cries of the oppressed or lets a violent predator walk free. We wouldn't call that judge "loving"; we would call him corrupt. God's judgment is His "no" to everything that destroys His creation. It is His holy commitment to set the world right. Because God is holy, He must oppose sin. Because He is just, He must punish it. Judgment is the proof that our lives—and our choices—actually matter. If there were no judgment, then ultimate evil and ultimate good would meet the same end, and the universe would be fundamentally meaningless.

What Is the "Fear of the Lord"?

When the Bible tells us to "fear God," it doesn't mean we should cower like a slave before a cruel and unpredictable master. The "fear of the Lord" is a profound sense of awe, reverence, and taking God seriously. It is the realization that we are finite and He is infinite; we are the creatures, and He is the Creator.

Fearing God means recognizing that His opinion of our lives carries more weight than the opinions of our peers, our culture, or even our own hearts. It is the "beginning of wisdom" because it aligns us with reality. If we don't fear God, we will inevitably fear everything else—the loss of money, the judgment of people, or the reality of death. But when we fear God, we are set free from every other fear. As the old saying goes: "He who fears God need fear no one else."

The Reality of Eternal Consequence

The Bible speaks with startling clarity about a coming day of judgment. It teaches that every hidden thought, every whispered word, and every private deed will be brought into the light of God's presence. This judgment is not just about a list of "bad things" we have done, but about the "debt" of rebellion we discussed in Chapter 25.

Because our sin is an offense against an eternal, infinitely holy God, the consequences are eternal. The Bible uses sobering metaphors—like "outer darkness," "the second death," or "separation"—to describe the outcome for those who persistently reject the Source of Life. God does not "send" people to judgment so much as He eventually honors their choice to live independently of Him. Judgment is God finally saying to the rebel, "Your will be done." It is the tragic fulfillment of a life lived in "Self-Sovereignty."

The Turning Point: Seeking Mercy

If the story ended with judgment, we would all be left in the dark. But the same God who is "Just" is also the "Justifier." He is a God who delights in showing mercy.

Mercy is not God "changing His mind" about the seriousness of sin; it is God providing a way for the penalty of sin to be paid by someone else. Mercy is God's "yes" to the sinner who stops making excuses, stops hiding in the bushes like Adam, and starts seeking help. To seek mercy is to cast yourself entirely on the character of God, trusting that He is "gracious and merciful, slow to anger and abounding in steadfast love" (Psalm 145:8). It is the act of a beggar coming to a King and finding a Father.

The Intersection of Justice and Mercy at the Cross

How can God be both perfectly just (demanding that sin be punished) and perfectly merciful (forgiving the sinner)? This is the central "knot" of the Bible, and it is untied only at the Cross of Jesus Christ.

At the Cross, the judgment we deserved was poured out on the Son. God did not ignore the debt; He paid it Himself. Justice was satisfied because sin was punished in Christ. Mercy was extended because we are offered the righteousness of Christ. In this singular "special act" of history, Justice and Mercy met and kissed. When we seek mercy through Christ, we aren't asking God to be unfair; we are asking Him to look at what Jesus did on our behalf. The Cross is the only place where we can see the full weight of God's wrath and the full height of His love at the exact same time.

Living in the Healthy Tension

Following God means living in the tension of fearing Him and trusting His mercy.

> **Fear keeps us from presumption:** It reminds us that sin is serious and God is not to be trifled with. It keeps us from "cheap grace"—the idea that we can live however we want because God "has to" forgive us.

> **Mercy keeps us from despair:** It reminds us that we are loved more than we can imagine. It tells us that our failures, no matter how great, are not the final word on our lives if we are in Christ.

When these two work together, they produce "Godly sorrow"—a grief over sin that leads to life-changing repentance, rather than a worldly shame that leads to hiding. We live with a "reverent confidence," trembling at His holiness while resting in His embrace.

Weekly Belief Statement

We believe that God is the holy and righteous Judge of all the earth, who will bring every work into judgment, whether good or evil. We affirm that His wrath against sin is just, necessary, and eternal. We also believe that God is rich in mercy and has provided a way of escape through the substitutionary sacrifice of His Son, Jesus Christ. We commit to living in the fear of the Lord, while resting entirely and joyfully in His merciful grace.

Practical Application

✟ **Acknowledge the Weight:** Spend a few minutes in silence today thinking about one area where you have "minimized" your sin. Instead of making excuses ("I was just tired"), name it before God and acknowledge that it truly deserves His judgment.

✟ **Run to the Mercy Seat:** After acknowledging your sin, immediately claim the mercy of God in Christ. Say: "Lord, I deserve Your judgment for this, but I thank You for Your mercy in Jesus." Don't wallow in guilt; walk in the freedom of being forgiven.

✟ **Practice Holy Awe:** Spend time outside looking at the stars, the ocean, or a vast landscape. Let the scale of creation remind you of the "bigness" of the Judge. Practice "fearing" Him by being amazed by His power.

✟ **Read the Warning and the Promise:** Read Matthew 10:28-31. Notice how Jesus tells us clearly whom we should fear (God), but immediately follows it with the tender reminder of how much the Father cares for even the smallest sparrow.

✟ **Pray for the Lost:** Think of someone you know who lives without a fear of God. Instead of feeling superior or judging them, pray that the Holy Spirit would open their eyes to the reality of judgment and the beauty of the mercy that is available to them.

"But with you there is forgiveness, that you may be feared." - Psalm 130:4

CHAPTER 28
Receive God's Grace Through His Covenants

In the shadow of the Fall and the weight of coming judgment, the human story could have easily ended in a dark silence. But God did not leave us to wander in the ruins of our own rebellion. Instead, He began to speak. He initiated a series of formal, solemn, and life-changing agreements called **Covenants**.

This chapter explores how God uses covenants to deliver His grace to a broken world. We will see that a covenant is more than just a contract; it is a bond of "sovereign administration." It is God's way of saying, "I will be your God, and you will be my people." When we understand the covenants, we see that God's grace is not a random feeling, but a rock-solid commitment woven through the fabric of history.

What is a Covenant?

In our world, we understand contracts. A contract is an agreement where two people trade services: "I will do this if you do that." But a biblical covenant is different. It is a relationship established by a king with his subjects, or a father with his children.

A covenant is a promise with a "sign" and a "seal." It is God binding Himself to His people. Even when we are unfaithful, God remains faithful to His covenant because His own name and reputation are on the line. Throughout the Bible, God unfolds His grace through several key covenants, each one building on the last like the chapters of a great rescue story.

The Covenant with Noah: Grace for the World

After the flood, God made a covenant with Noah, his family, and every living creature. He promised never again to destroy the earth with a flood.

✠ **The Grace:** This is "common grace." It ensures that the seasons will continue and the earth will remain stable so that the story of redemption can move forward.

✠ **The Sign:** The Rainbow. Every time we see a rainbow, we are reminded that God is a promise-keeper who preserves the world even when it is sinful.

The Covenant with Abraham: Grace Through a Family

God then called a man named Abraham and made a staggering promise: through Abraham's family, all the nations of the earth would be blessed.

✠ **The Grace:** This is "choosing grace." God picked one family to be the vehicle of His salvation. He promised Abraham land, a multitude of descendants, and a "Seed" who would eventually crush the serpent.

✠ **The Sign:** Circumcision. This was a physical mark that set God's people apart and reminded them that they belonged to Him.

The Covenant with Moses: Grace Through the Law

At Mount Sinai, God gave the law to the nation of Israel. While we often think of the law as "rules," it was actually given in the context of a covenant. God first saved them from Egypt, and *then* He gave them the law.

✠ **The Grace:** This is "guiding grace." The covenant showed Israel how to live as a "kingdom of priests" in a dark world. It provided the Tabernacle and the sacrificial system, showing that God wanted to dwell in the midst of His people, even though they were sinners.

✠ **The Sign:** The Sabbath. By resting, Israel showed the world that they trusted in God's provision rather than their own effort.

The Covenant with David: Grace Through a King

Centuries later, God promised King David that one of his descendants would sit on the throne forever.

✠ **The Grace:** This is "ruling grace." It pointed to a future King who would bring perfect justice and peace. This covenant narrowed the search for the Savior: He wouldn't just be a human (from Noah), or a Hebrew (from Abraham); He would be a King from the line of David.

The New Covenant: The Climax of Grace

All these earlier covenants were pointing toward the "New Covenant" promised by the prophets and inaugurated by Jesus. At the Last Supper, Jesus held up the cup and said, "This cup is the new covenant in my blood" (Luke 22:20).

✝ **The Grace:** This is "completing grace." In the New Covenant, the law is written on our hearts (internal transformation), our sins are remembered no more (total forgiveness), and we all "know the Lord" personally.

✝ **The Mediator:** Jesus is the "Guarantee" of this covenant. He fulfilled the requirements that we failed to keep. He took the "curse" of the broken covenants so that we could receive the "blessing" of the new one.

How We Receive the Grace

Covenants are not just ancient history; they are the way we relate to God today. We don't come to God based on our daily performance; we come to Him based on the **Covenant of Grace**.

When you feel like a failure, you don't have to wonder if God has abandoned you. You can look at the "blood of the eternal covenant" and know that His commitment to you is based on Jesus' work, not your own. Receiving this grace means trusting that God is a "Covenant-Keeper." It means resting in the fact that He has legally and lovingly bound Himself to you.

Weekly Belief Statement

We believe that God has graciously initiated a series of covenants throughout history to reveal His plan of salvation. We affirm that while humanity has broken every promise, God has remained faithful to His covenant word. We believe that all the biblical covenants find their "Yes" and "Amen" in Jesus Christ, who has established the New Covenant through His death and resurrection for the forgiveness of our sins.

Practical Application

✝ **Look for the Signs:** This week, when you see a rainbow or observe a day of rest (Sabbath), stop and specifically thank God for His covenant faithfulness. Remind yourself: "My God keeps His word."

✝ **Identify the Roots:** Read Genesis 12:1–3. Notice how God's promise to Abraham covers your life today as a follower of Christ. You are part of that "blessing to the nations."

✝ **Pray the New Covenant:** Read Jeremiah 31:31–34. Turn it into a prayer: "Lord, write Your law on my heart today. Help me to know You more deeply."

✝ **Rest in the Mediator:** When you feel the "fear of judgment" (from Chapter 27), remind yourself that Jesus is your Covenant Advocate. He has already paid the "penalty clause" of the law for you.

✝ **Examine the Cup:** The next time you take the Lord's Supper (Communion), listen closely to the words "the new covenant in my blood." Realize that you are participating in a legal, binding, and loving agreement with the King of the Universe.

"Now may the God of peace, who through the blood of the eternal covenant brought back from the dead our Lord Jesus, that great Shepherd of the sheep, 21 equip you with everything good for doing his will, and may he work in us what is pleasing to him, through Jesus Christ, to whom be glory for ever and ever. Amen." - Hebrews 13:20–21

PART SIX
Look to Christ

CHAPTER 29
Confess Jesus Christ as Fully God and Fully Man

As we move into Part 6 of our map, we come to the mystery that holds the entire Christian faith together. We have seen the problem of sin and the promise of the covenants; now we meet the Person who fulfills it all. The central claim of Christianity is not just that a good teacher appeared in Israel, but that God Himself "tabernacled" among us.

This chapter explores the **Incarnation**—the act of the eternal Son of God taking on a human nature. We will look at the two natures of Jesus: His full deity and His full humanity. To confess Jesus as "God-Man" is not just a theological riddle; it is the only way our salvation is possible. If He were only God, He could not represent us. If He were only man, He could not save us. In Jesus, we find the bridge that spans the infinite gap.

Fully God: The Eternal Son

The New Testament leaves no room for the idea that Jesus was merely a human prophet. From the opening lines of John's Gospel, we are told that "the Word was God" (John 1:1). Throughout His ministry, Jesus did things that only God has the right to do.

✝ **He Forgave Sins:** When Jesus told the paralytic his sins were forgiven, the religious leaders rightly asked, "Who can forgive sins but God alone?" (Mark 2:7).

✝ **He Accepted Worship:** While angels and apostles always refused worship, Jesus accepted it from Thomas, the blind man, and His disciples.

✝ **He Claimed the Divine Name:** Jesus told the crowds, "Before Abraham was, I AM" (John 8:58), using the sacred name God gave to Moses at the burning bush.

As the "radiance of the glory of God and the exact imprint of his nature" (Hebrews 1:3), Jesus possesses all the attributes of deity. He is all-knowing, all-powerful, and eternal. When we look at Jesus, we are not looking at a "version" of God; we are looking at God Himself.

Fully Man: The Shared Brother

At the same time, Jesus was not a ghost or a god "disguised" as a human. He was, and is, fully human. The "Word became flesh" (John 1:14). This means He didn't just have a human body; He had a human mind, human emotions, and a human will.

✝ **He Was Born:** He entered the world through a human mother.

✝ **He Grew:** He increased in wisdom and stature (Luke 2:52).

✝ **He Suffered:** He felt hunger, thirst, fatigue, and physical agony.

✝ **He Wept:** He experienced the depth of human grief and sorrow.

Jesus had to be fully man to be our **Mediator**. To pay the debt of humanity, the Savior had to *be* a human. Because He has lived our life, He is not a distant judge, but a "high priest" who is able to sympathize with our weaknesses (Hebrews 4:15).

Two Natures, One Person

The church has historically used the term "Hypostatic Union" to describe how this works. It means that Jesus is not "half-god and half-man." He is 100% God and 100% man. These two natures are joined together in one Person without being mixed or changed.

Imagine a heated iron bar. It has the nature of iron (solid, heavy) and the nature of fire (hot, glowing). They are distinct natures, but they occupy the same space and work together. In a far greater way, Jesus operates with the power of God and the heart of a man. This union is permanent; Jesus rose from the dead in a human body, and He sits at the right hand of the Father today as the glorified God-Man.

Why This Matters for You

Why is this doctrine worth "confessing" with such passion? Because it is the foundation of your security.

1. **The Sacrifice is Sufficient:** Because He is God, His death on the cross has infinite value. It is enough to cover the sins of the whole world for all time.

2. **The Representation is Perfect:** Because He is man, He can stand in our place. He is the "Second Adam" who succeeded where the first Adam failed.

3. **The Access is Open:** Because He is both, He holds the hand of the Father and the hand of humanity. He is the only bridge. As 1 Timothy 2:5 says, "For there is one God, and there is one mediator between God and men, the man Christ Jesus."

The Humility of the Incarnation

The Incarnation is the ultimate example of humility. Paul tells us in Philippians 2 that Jesus did not consider His equality with God something to be "grasped" or used for His own advantage. Instead, He "emptied himself" by taking the form of a servant.

Confessing Jesus as God and man challenges our pride. If the King of the universe was willing to put on the "apron" of humanity to wash our feet and die for our sins, we cannot live lives of arrogance. To follow the God-Man is to embrace a life of humble service.

Weekly Belief Statement

We believe that our Lord Jesus Christ is the eternal Son of God, who for us and for our salvation became truly man. We confess that He is fully God and fully man—two distinct natures in one Person—conceived by the Holy Spirit and born of the Virgin Mary. We believe He is the only Mediator who can represent us before God and satisfy divine justice on our behalf.

Practical Application

✝ **Marvel at the Mystery:** Spend five minutes today thinking about this: the One who created the stars once slept in a wooden manger. Let the "bigness" and "nearness" of Jesus fill you with awe.

✝ **Talk to the Sympathetic Priest:** When you feel overwhelmed or tempted this week, remember that Jesus has felt it too. Instead of hiding, tell Him: "Lord, You know what this feels like. Please help me."

✝ **Read the Narrative:** Read the first two chapters of Luke. Pay attention to the "divine" announcements and the "human" details of the birth of Jesus.

✝ **Defend the Truth:** If someone tells you Jesus was "just a good teacher," practice explaining why He had to be God to save us and man to represent us.

✝ **Imitate the Humility:** Identify one area where you are insisting on your "rights" or your "status." Look at the example of the Incarnation and choose to serve instead.

"And the Word became flesh and dwelt among us, and we have seen his glory, glory as of the only Son from the Father, full of grace and truth." - John 1:14

CHAPTER 30
Trust Jesus' Perfect Life for Your Righteousness

When we think about the work of Jesus, our minds almost instinctively go to the Cross. We think of His death as the moment our sins were washed away, and rightly so. However, if Jesus had only died for us, we would be like a debtor whose debt was canceled but who still has zero dollars in his bank account. We would be "neutral", not guilty, but not necessarily "righteous" either.

This chapter explores why the **life** of Jesus matters just as much as His death. To be accepted by a holy God, we don't just need our "badness" removed; we need a "goodness" that matches God's perfect standard. We need what theologians call the **Active Obedience of Christ.** When we trust in Jesus, God doesn't just see a forgiven sinner; He sees someone who has perfectly kept every law, because Jesus did it in our place.

The Problem of Passive Neutrality

Imagine you are standing before a judge for a massive debt. Someone steps in and pays every penny. You walk out of the courtroom free—but you are still broke. You have no "credit" to buy a home, start a life, or enter the King's palace.

The Moral Law of God (which we studied in Chapter 24) requires two things:

1. **The Penalty for Disobedience:** Death (which Jesus paid).
2. **The Requirement of Perfect Obedience:** Life (which Jesus lived).

If we want to live with God forever, we need a "perfect score" on the test of life. Since we have already failed that test, we need someone to take it for us.

The Second Adam: Succeeding Where We Failed

To understand Jesus' life, we have to look back at the first Adam in the Garden. Adam was given a choice to obey, and he failed, plunging humanity into sin. Jesus is called the "Last Adam" (1 Corinthians 15:45).

Where the first Adam was tempted in a lush garden and gave in, Jesus was tempted in a barren wilderness and stood firm. Where Israel failed to keep the law for forty years in the desert, Jesus was faithful for forty days of testing. Throughout His thirty-three years on earth, Jesus lived a life of "uninterrupted" holiness. Every thought, every word, and every hidden motive was perfectly aligned with the Father's will.

The Great Exchange: His Record for Yours

The heart of the Gospel is a "Great Exchange." In this exchange, our sin was placed on Jesus at the Cross, and **His righteousness is placed on us through faith.** The Apostle Paul describes this in 2 Corinthians 5:21: "For our sake he made him to be sin who knew no sin, so that in him we might become the righteousness of God." Notice it doesn't say we just become "innocent"; it says we become "the righteousness of God." When God looks at a believer, He "imputes" (credits) the perfect life of Jesus to that person's account.

Why the Virgin Birth Matters

This perfect life was possible only because of the **Virgin Birth**. As we touched on in the previous chapter, Jesus had to be born of a woman to be human, but conceived by the Holy Spirit to be free from the "inherited sin" of Adam.

If Jesus had been born in the natural way, He would have been born "under the debt" of sin like the rest of us. He would have needed a Savior for Himself. But because He was conceived by the Spirit, He was the only human being since the Fall to start with a "clean slate." He was the only one capable of living a life that could be offered as a perfect substitute for others.

Resting in His Performance, Not Yours

Most people spend their lives on a "treadmill of performance." We try to be "good enough" to make God like us. We think that if we pray enough, give enough, or stay moral enough, God will accept us. But the standard is not "good enough"; the standard is **perfection.**

Trusting in Jesus' perfect life means getting off the treadmill. It means realizing that you can never be righteous enough to earn heaven, but Jesus has already been righteous enough for you.

✝ When you feel like a failure, you remember **His** success.

✝ When your conscience accuses you of being "not enough," you point to **His** "it is finished."

✝ When you fear God's judgment, you realize the Father loves you with the same love He has for His perfect Son.

The Motivation for Holiness

Does this mean we stop trying to live holy lives? Not at all! But our motivation changes. We don't obey to **get** a standing with God; we obey because we already **have** a standing with God.

Because we have been credited with Jesus' perfect life, we now want to live in a way that reflects who we are in Him. We aren't working *for* life; we are working *from* life. This is the only kind of obedience that is fueled by love and gratitude rather than fear and pride.

Weekly Belief Statement

We believe that Jesus Christ lived a life of perfect, sinless obedience to the Father's will in our place. We affirm that His righteousness is credited to every believer by grace through faith alone. We believe that we are accepted by God not because of our own performance, but because of the perfect performance of Jesus Christ, our Substitute and our Savior.

Practical Application

✝ **Confess the "Treadmill":** Identify one area where you are trying to "earn" God's favor (e.g., "If I read my Bible every day, God will bless my business"). Repent of that legalism and thank Jesus for His perfect record.

✝ **The Morning Identity Check:** Before you start your day, say to yourself: "Today, God's favor on me is not based on how well I do, but on how well Jesus did." Notice how this reduces your anxiety.

✝ **Read the "Active" Obedience:** Read Hebrews 4:14–16. Reflect on the fact that Jesus was "tempted in every way as we are, yet without sin." Thank Him for staying faithful when you were not.

✝ **Look at the "Garments":** Read the parable of the wedding feast in Matthew 22:1–14. Pay attention to the "wedding garment" provided by the King. Realize that Jesus' righteousness is the only "garment" that allows us to stay at the feast.

✝ **Respond with Gratitude:** Choose one difficult command of God (like "love your enemy") and attempt it today, not to prove you are good, but as a "thank you" note to the One who was perfectly good for you.

"For as by the one man's disobedience the many were made sinners, so by the one man's obedience the many will be made righteous." - Romans 5:19

CHAPTER 31
Rely on the Cross and Christ's Saving Work

We now come to the physical and spiritual center of the Christian faith: the Cross. While we have looked at the beauty of Jesus' life and the mystery of His birth, everything in the "Map of Reality" has been leading to this moment. The Cross is not just a tragic end to a noble life; it is the most significant event in the history of the universe. It is the place where the love of God and the justice of God met to accomplish our rescue.

In this chapter, we explore what actually happened when Jesus was hung on that Roman instrument of death. We will see that the Cross was a sacrifice, a payment, and a victory. When we learn to rely on the work of Christ rather than our own efforts, we find the only foundation that can support the weight of our souls.

The Problem the Cross Solved

To understand the Cross, we must remember the problem of sin we discussed in Part 5. We owed a debt we could not pay, and we stood under a judgment we could not escape. Because God is perfectly holy, He cannot simply overlook sin; it must be dealt with.

If God were to forgive sin without a penalty being paid, He would no longer be just. If He were to execute justice without providing a way of escape, we would all be lost. The Cross is God's brilliant and costly solution. On the Cross, God did not bypass His justice; He satisfied it by taking the penalty upon Himself.

Substitution: He Stood in Our Place

The heart of the Cross is **substitution**. This means that Jesus did not die for His own sins (He had none), but for ours. He was our "Substitute."

The Bible uses the word *propitiation* to describe this. It means a sacrifice that turns away wrath. On the Cross, Jesus became the "lightning rod" for the judgment that was headed toward us. He took the "cup" of

God's righteous anger against sin and drank it to the very last drop. When He cried out, "It is finished," He meant that the debt was paid in full. There is nothing left for you to pay.

Redemption: He Bought Us Back

Another way the Bible describes the Cross is through the language of the marketplace: **redemption**. To redeem something means to buy it back or to pay a ransom to set someone free.

Because of sin, we were "slaves to sin" and "captives" to the power of darkness. We were like prisoners in a cell we could not unlock. By shedding His blood, Jesus paid the "ransom price" to buy us out of that slavery. We no longer belong to our past, our failures, or the enemy; we belong to the One who bought us at the highest possible price.

Reconciliation: He Brought Us Home

Finally, the Cross accomplished **reconciliation**. As we saw in the Fall, sin created a massive "divide" between us and God. We were alienated, distant, and—spiritually speaking—at war with our Creator.

The Cross tore down the curtain that separated us from God. Because the obstacle of sin has been removed, the way is now open for us to come home. Reconciliation means that the "war" is over. For those who rely on Christ, there is no longer a barrier between them and the Father. We can walk into His presence with the confidence of children.

The Victory of the Cross

It is easy to look at the Cross and see only weakness and defeat. But the Bible presents the Cross as a moment of supreme victory. Colossians 2:15 tells us that on the Cross, Jesus "disarmed the rulers and authorities and put them to open shame, by triumphing over them in him."

By dying, Jesus took away the enemy's only weapon: the legal claim that our sin gives him over our lives. Since the debt is paid, the "accuser" has nothing left to say. The Cross was the "crushing of the serpent's head" that was promised in the Garden.

How to Rely on the Cross

Relying on the Cross is more than just believing it happened; it is a posture of the heart.

 Stop Trying to Pay: Many people spend their lives trying to "make up" for their sins through good works. This is an insult to the Cross. If you could pay for your sins, Jesus wouldn't have had to die.

✢ **Look Away from Yourself:** Your security does not come from the strength of your faith, but from the object of your faith. When you feel guilty, don't look at your own "record"; look at the Cross.

✢ **Live in the "Done":** Most religions are based on "Do." Christianity is based on "Done." Relying on the Cross means waking up every day and realizing that the most important work of your life has already been finished by someone else.

Weekly Belief Statement

We believe that Jesus Christ died on the cross as a perfect and sufficient sacrifice for the sins of the world. We affirm that He died in our place, bearing the judgment we deserved and paying the debt we could not pay. We believe that through His blood, we are redeemed from slavery to sin and reconciled to God, and we rest entirely in His finished work for our salvation.

Practical Application

✢ **Confess the "Payment Plan":** Identify one way you try to "pay God back" for your mistakes (extra prayers, self-criticism, etc.). Stop that practice today and simply say, "Jesus, Your death was enough."

✢ **Look at the Symbol:** This week, whenever you see a cross (on a building, jewelry, or in a book), let it be a 5-second "trigger" for gratitude. Say, "Thank You, Lord, for standing in my place."

✢ **Read the Account:** Read Mark 15. Read it slowly, putting yourself in the scene. Realize that every drop of blood was shed with *you* in mind.

✢ **Declare the Victory:** When you feel "accused" by your past mistakes this week, tell your heart: "The debt is paid. The case is closed. Jesus has won."

✢ **Carry the Cross:** Jesus told us to "take up our cross" and follow Him. Think of one area where you can sacrificially serve someone else this week as a small reflection of the great sacrifice Jesus made for you.

"May I never boast except in the cross of our Lord Jesus Christ, through which the world has been crucified to me, and I to the world." - Galatians 6:14

CHAPTER 32
Celebrate the Resurrection as Your Living Hope

If the story of Jesus had ended at the tomb, we might remember Him as a tragic hero, a great teacher, or a martyr for a noble cause. But we would not worship Him as Savior. Without the Resurrection, the Cross would be a place of defeat, and our faith would be, as the Apostle Paul bluntly put it, "in vain" (1 Corinthians 15:14).

This chapter explores the historical reality and the spiritual power of Jesus rising from the dead. The Resurrection is the "Amen" to everything Jesus claimed and did. It is the receipt showing that the check He wrote on the Cross has cleared the bank of Heaven. When we celebrate the Resurrection, we aren't just cheering for a past miracle; we are standing on a "living hope" that changes how we face life, death, and the future.

The Fact of the Resurrection

The Christian faith is not built on a "spiritual feeling" or a metaphor, but on a physical event that happened in a specific place at a specific time.

- **The Empty Tomb:** The body of Jesus was gone. Despite the Roman guard and the sealed stone, the tomb could not hold the Author of Life.

- **The Eyewitnesses:** Jesus didn't just appear to one or two people in a dark room. He appeared to Mary Magdalene, the twelve apostles, and at one point, more than 500 people at once (1 Corinthians 15:6). He ate food with them and invited them to touch His scars to prove He wasn't a ghost.

- **The Transformed Apostles:** The same men who ran away in fear on Friday were willing to die for their testimony a few weeks later. They didn't die for a "beautiful idea"; they died because they had seen the risen Lord.

The Vindication of the Son

The Resurrection was God the Father's public "stamp of approval" on the work of Jesus. On the Cross, Jesus was "reckoned among the transgressors" (Isaiah 53:12). To the world, He looked like a criminal rejected by God.

But by raising Him from the dead, God vindicated Jesus. The Resurrection proved that:

1. **Jesus is who He said He was:** The Son of God.

2. **The Sacrifice worked:** Death had no more legal claim on Him because the debt of sin had been fully paid.

3. **The Father was satisfied:** The work of redemption was complete.

The Defeat of the Last Enemy

In Chapter 26, we saw that death is the "great interrupter" that broke the world. It is the one enemy that every human, regardless of wealth or power, must eventually face.

The Resurrection is the "death of death." By going into the grave and coming out the other side, Jesus broke the power of the tomb. He now holds "the keys of Death and Hades" (Revelation 1:18). For the believer, death has been transformed from a "dead end" into a "doorway." Because He lives, we also will live. The Resurrection is the "firstfruits"—the promise that what happened to Jesus' body will one day happen to ours.

A Living Hope for Today

The Resurrection isn't just about what happens after we die; it's about a "living hope" right now. A living hope is a hope that has "breath in its lungs." It is active and energizing.

✞ **Power for Change:** The same power that raised Jesus from the dead is now at work within every believer (Ephesians 1:19-20). This means we are not stuck in our old patterns of sin and despair. New life is possible.

✞ **Purpose in Suffering:** Because of the Resurrection, we know that the "brokenness" of this world (Chapter 21) is temporary. Every tear will be redeemed, and every loss will be restored.

✞ **Confidence in Prayer:** We don't pray to a dead memory; we talk to a living, reigning King who is currently interceding for us at the right hand of the Father.

The New Creation Has Begun

The Resurrection was the "Big Bang" of the New Creation. It was the first square inch of the world being put back right. When Jesus stepped out of the tomb, the "thorns and thistles" of the Fall began to retreat.

As followers of the Risen Christ, we are called to be "Resurrection people." We live as citizens of the world to come. We work for justice, we show mercy, and we create beauty because we know that in Christ, "nothing you do in the Lord is in vain" (1 Corinthians 15:58). The end of the story has been written, and it is a story of life winning over death.

Weekly Belief Statement

We believe that Jesus Christ was physically raised from the dead on the third day, according to the Scriptures. We affirm that His resurrection is the victory over sin and death and the guarantee of our own future resurrection. We believe that He is the Living Lord who gives us a living hope, and we rejoice that He is making all things new.

Practical Application

✝ **Audit Your Fears:** What is the "worst-case scenario" you are currently afraid of? Remind yourself that even if that happened, the Resurrection means that death and loss do not have the final word.

✝ **The "He is Risen" Greeting:** Even if it isn't Easter, take a moment this week to tell another believer, "Christ is risen!" Let the reality of that fact settle into your conversation.

✝ **Read the Resurrection Accounts:** Read 1 Corinthians 15. It is the "resurrection chapter" of the Bible. Note how many times Paul connects Jesus' rising to our daily life and future hope.

✝ **Invest in the Eternal:** Since the Resurrection proves that the physical world matters and will be redeemed, do one "good work" this week, like helping a neighbor or cleaning a park, as a way of honoring the God who restores His creation.

✝ **Talk to the Living King:** In your prayers this week, start by acknowledging that Jesus is alive and present with you. Shift from "asking for things" to "relating to a Person."

CHAPTER 33
Submit to Christ's Reign Right Now

Many people are comfortable with Jesus as a "Savior", the one who forgives their past and secures their future. We love the idea of the baby in the manger or the Savior on the Cross. But the Bible presents a further, even more encompassing reality: the **Ascension**. After His resurrection, Jesus didn't just disappear; He ascended into heaven to take His seat at the right hand of God the Father.

This chapter explores what theologians call the "Session" of Christ, His current, active reign as King of the universe. To submit to Christ's reign right now is to recognize that He is not just a figure from history or a future hope, but the sitting Sovereign over every square inch of your life today.

The Coronation: The Meaning of the Ascension

The Ascension was more than a spectacular exit; it was a royal coronation. When Jesus sat down at the right hand of the Father, it signaled that His work of *atonement* was finished and His work of *ruling* had begun.

In the ancient world, the "right hand" was the position of highest authority and power. It means Jesus is the Father's "Prime Minister," executing the divine will across the cosmos. Before He ascended, Jesus declared, "All authority in heaven and on earth has been given to me" (Matthew 28:18). There is no person, government, or spiritual power that is not ultimately accountable to Him. He is the "King of Kings", the one to whom every other earthly authority must eventually answer.

Christ as Prophet, Priest, and King

From His throne, Jesus continues to fulfill three "offices" or roles in the life of the believer. Understanding these helps us know how to submit to Him:

1. **Our Prophet:** He continues to speak to us through His Word (the Bible) and His Spirit. We submit to His reign by listening to His voice above the noise of the culture. When we prioritize Scripture over secular wisdom, we are acknowledging Him as our Prophet.

2. **Our Priest:** He is not a distant, cold monarch. Hebrews 7:25 tells us He "always lives to make intercession" for us. Even now, He is representing your needs and your name before the Father. We submit by bringing our requests to Him, trusting His advocacy rather than our own merit.

3. **Our King:** He governs our hearts by His grace and protects us from our spiritual enemies. He is the one who "orders all things for the good of those who love him." We submit by obeying His commands, even when they are difficult.

The "Crown Rights" Over All of Life

A famous theologian once said, "There is not a square inch in the whole domain of our human existence over which Christ, who is Sovereign over all, does not cry: 'Mine!'"

Submitting to Christ's reign right now means acknowledging His "crown rights" over every area of your life. He is not just King of your "spiritual life" or your Sunday mornings. He is King over:

✝ **Your Money:** He owns the gold and the silver. We are merely managers of His resources.

✝ **Your Relationships:** He dictates how we treat our spouses, our children, and our enemies. We do not have the right to hold grudges when the King commands forgiveness.

✝ **Your Work:** Whether you are a teacher, a builder, or a parent, you work for the King. Excellence in our tasks is an act of royal service.

✝ **Your Body:** As the King who bought you with His blood, He has the right to determine how you treat the "temple" of your body.

Living as a Citizen of the Kingdom

We often live as if we are the kings of our own little islands. We want to be the ones who decide what is right and wrong, what is important and what is a waste of time. But to follow Jesus is to change citizenship. We are now "ambassadors" of a different Kingdom.

Submitting to His reign means we no longer ask, "What do I want to do?" but "What does my King command?" This isn't a burdensome slavery; it is the freedom of being under the protection of a perfectly wise and loving Ruler. When we submit to Him, we stop carrying the weight of trying to run the world ourselves. We can sleep at night because the King is awake and on His throne.

The Conflict of Kingdoms

We must recognize that Christ's reign is currently "already but not yet" fully visible. While He is the legal King of the world, there are still many "rebels" (including parts of our own hearts) that refuse to bow.

We live in a time of spiritual tension. Every act of obedience, every word of truth, and every deed of mercy is an act of "resistance" against the kingdom of darkness. We submit to Christ's reign by choosing to live by the laws of Heaven while we are still residents of earth. We don't wait for the world to recognize Him before we begin to obey Him. We live now as we will live then.

Weekly Belief Statement

We believe that Jesus Christ ascended into heaven and is seated at the right hand of God the Father Almighty. We affirm that He is the King of kings and Lord of lords, possessing all authority in heaven and on earth. We believe that He currently reigns over all things for the sake of His Church, and we commit to submitting every area of our lives, our thoughts, our resources, and our actions, to His sovereign and gracious rule.

Practical Application

- **The "Square Inch" Audit:** Identify one area of your life (e.g., your social media use, your hobbies, your secret thoughts) where you have been acting as the "King." Formally "hand over the keys" to Jesus in prayer today.

- **Practice "Immediate Obedience":** This week, when you feel the Holy Spirit prompting you to do something (like apologize to someone or give generously), do it immediately. Treat it as a direct order from your King rather than a suggestion.

- **Read the Royal Psalms:** Read Psalm 2 or Psalm 110. Notice the power and authority of the promised King. Reflect on the fact that this King is the same one who washed the feet of His disciples.

✝ **Pray for the Kingdom:** When you pray the Lord's Prayer ("Your kingdom come, your will be done"), focus on your local community. Ask Jesus to manifest His reign of justice and peace in your specific neighborhood.

✝ **Acknowledge the Intercessor:** When you feel guilty or "not enough" this week, remember that your King is also your Priest. Visualize Him standing before the Father, speaking on your behalf, ensuring that your place in the Kingdom is secure.

"He must reign until he has put all his enemies under his feet." - 1 Corinthians 15:25

CHAPTER 34
Watch for Christ's Return

The story of the Bible does not end with the Church struggling in a broken world, nor does it end with the Ascension of Jesus into a distant heaven. It ends with a homecoming. Every theme we have traced through this "Map of Reality", from the perfection of creation to the tragedy of the Fall, and from the blood of the covenants to the victory of the Resurrection, reaches its final crescendo in the **Second Coming of Jesus Christ.**

This chapter explores the "Blessed Hope" of the Christian faith. To watch for Christ's return is not about chart-making or sensational predictions; it is about a posture of the heart. It is the steady, joyful expectation that the King who left will one day return to finish what He started. When we live in light of His return, our priorities shift, our hope anchors, and our perseverance deepens.

The Certainty of the Promise

The return of Jesus is not a peripheral doctrine or a piece of "fan fiction" added to the end of the Gospels. It is one of the most frequently mentioned truths in the New Testament. Just as the prophets of the Old Testament looked forward to the first coming of the Messiah, the apostles of the New Testament look forward to His second appearing.

When Jesus ascended (Chapter 33), two angels stood by the disciples and gave a clear promise: "This Jesus, who was taken up from you into heaven, will come in the same way as you saw him go into heaven" (Acts 1:11). Jesus Himself told His followers, "I will come again and will take you to myself" (John 14:3). The return of Christ is as certain as His first breath in the manger and His last breath on the Cross. It is the "Amen" of history.

What Will the Return Be Like?

While there has been much debate over the specific timing and sequence of end-time events, the Bible gives us several clear characteristics of Christ's return that all believers can agree on:

1. **It Will Be Personal and Physical:** Jesus is not returning as a "spirit" or a "vague influence." The same Jesus who ate fish with the disciples and showed them His scars will return in a physical body.

2. **It Will Be Visible and Universal:** It won't be a secret event. As lightning flashes from the east to the west, so will be the coming of the Son of Man. Every eye will see Him.

3. **It Will Be Sudden and Unexpected:** Jesus warned that He would come like a "thief in the night." While there are signs to watch for, the exact day and hour are known only to the Father.

4. **It Will Be Glorious:** At His first coming, Jesus came in humility and weakness. At His second coming, He will come in power and great glory, leading the armies of heaven to execute final justice and establish His visible kingdom.

The Purpose of His Return: Completion

Why must Jesus return? He returns to complete the work of redemption in three specific ways:

✞ **The Resurrection of the Dead:** When Christ returns, the bodies of those who have died in Him will be raised and transformed into "glorious bodies" like His own. The "living hope" we discussed in Chapter 32 reaches its physical fulfillment.

✞ **The Final Judgment:** As we saw in Chapter 27, there must be a reckoning. Jesus will sit on His glorious throne and separate the sheep from the goats. He will right every wrong, silence every lie, and deal finally with the powers of darkness.

✞ **The New Creation:** Jesus does not return to destroy the world, but to "make all things new." He returns to merge heaven and earth, removing the curse of the Fall and establishing a world where "death shall be no more" (Revelation 21:4).

The Danger of Distraction

Because the return of Christ has been "delayed" in our eyes, it is easy to fall into what the Bible calls "spiritual slumber." We start to live as if this world is all there is. We begin to build our "castles in the sand," forgetting that the tide is coming in.

Jesus frequently told parables about servants who were left in charge while their master was away. The "wicked servant" is the one who says, "My master is delayed," and begins to live selfishly and recklessly. To "watch" is to resist the gravitational pull of worldliness. It is to keep our "lamps trimmed" and our hearts ready, knowing that we will one day give an account of how we used the time and talents He entrusted to us.

How to Watch: Active Waiting

Watching for Christ's return is not a passive activity. It isn't standing on a mountaintop staring at the sky. Biblical "watching" is **active**.

1. **Watchful Holiness:** We live in a way that we wouldn't be ashamed if He walked through the door at any moment. Peter asks, "Since all these things are thus to be dissolved, what sort of people ought you to be in lives of holiness and godliness?" (2 Peter 3:11).

2. **Watchful Mission:** Jesus said the Gospel must be proclaimed to all nations before the end comes. We watch for His return by being busy with His work, sharing the Good News and making disciples.

3. **Watchful Prayer:** We join the ancient cry of the Church: *Maranatha!* "Our Lord, come!" (1 Corinthians 16:22). We pray for His return because we love His appearing.

Hope in the Midst of Trials

For the suffering believer (Chapter 21), the return of Christ is the ultimate comfort. It means that the pain of the present is not the final word. It means that the "arc of the moral universe" does not just bend toward justice; it is pulled toward Justice by a Person.

When we face the "thorns and thistles" of a broken world, we look up. We realize that our King is on His way. This perspective allows us to endure hardship with a specific kind of "resurrection joy." We know that the dawn is coming, and that the "light momentary affliction" of this life is preparing for us an "eternal weight of glory."

Weekly Belief Statement

We believe that Jesus Christ will return to this earth personally, visibly, and gloriously to judge the living and the dead. We affirm the certain hope of the resurrection of the body and the final renewal of all creation. We believe that the return of Christ is the climax of the redemptive story, and we commit to living watchfully, holistically, and missionally as we await His appearing.

Practical Application

- **The "What If" Reflection:** Ask yourself honestly: "If Jesus returned this afternoon, what would I be doing? Is there anything in my life I would desperately want to hide or change?" Use that reflection to prompt immediate repentance.

- **Set Your Affections:** Spend time this week reading Revelation 21 and 22. Visualize the beauty of the New Creation. Let the "brightness" of that future dim the "glitter" of the world's temporary treasures.

- **Pray the Maranatha:** Make "Come, Lord Jesus" a part of your daily prayer rhythm this week. Especially when you see news of injustice or experience personal pain, use it as a trigger to ask for His return.

- **Be Occupied with the Mission:** Identify one person in your life who does not know the hope of Christ. Realizing that the time is short, pray for an opportunity to share the "Map of Reality" with them this week.

- **Live with "Eternal Investment":** Think of one way you can invest your time or money into something that will last beyond the return of Christ (e.g., teaching a child, helping a church, or serving the poor).

"He who testifies to these things says, 'Surely I am coming soon.' Amen. Come, Lord Jesus!" - Revelation 22:20

PART SEVEN
Receive Salvation and Walk in New Life

CHAPTER 35
Hear the Gospel Call and Respond

For a seed to grow, it must first be planted. In the same way, for salvation to take root in a human heart, the message of the Gospel must be heard. Throughout this book, we have explored the "content" of the Gospel: the facts of Christ's life, death, and resurrection. But in this chapter, we look at the "call" of the Gospel. This is the moment where the truth of God's Word moves from being general information to a personal invitation.

Hearing the Gospel call is the first step in what theologians call the *Ordo Salutis,* or the "Order of Salvation." It is the bridge between the finished work of Christ on the Cross and the practical application of that work to your own life. When we respond to this call, we aren't just agreeing with a set of historical facts; we are answering the voice of the King who is calling us by name.

The Two Dimensions of the Call

To understand how God "calls" us, we must look at the two distinct ways the Bible describes this process. One is a sound that hits everyone's ears; the other is a power that opens someone's heart.

1. The General (External) Call

The general call is the Gospel message being proclaimed to all people everywhere without exception. Whenever a preacher stands in a pulpit, a missionary travels to a distant village, or a friend shares their faith over coffee, the general call is going out.

God sincerely invites all people to turn to Him. He says in Isaiah 45:22, "Turn to me and be saved, all the ends of the earth!" This call is a genuine offer of mercy. It makes people accountable for how they respond to God's grace. However, the Bible and human experience both show that many people hear this call and reject it. They hear the words, but they do not see the beauty of the Savior.

2. The Effectual (Internal) Call

Have you ever heard a truth a hundred times, but then, in one specific moment, it finally "clicks"? It moves from being an abstract idea in your head to a burning reality in your heart. That is the internal call.

Theologians call this "effectual" because it actually achieves the effect it intends. It is the work of the Holy Spirit moving within a person to open their eyes, soften their "stony heart," and make the Gospel irresistible. While the external call is the work of man's voice, the internal call is the work of God's power. As Paul writes in 1 Corinthians 1:23-24, the Gospel is a "stumbling block" to some and "folly" to others, but to those who are *called*, it is the "power of God and the wisdom of God."

The Content of the Proclamation

If we are to be heralds of this call, we must be clear about its content. The Gospel call is not an invitation to "become a better person," "find your best life," or "join a social cause." It is a summons to a new reality that contains three essential elements:

- **A Declaration of Fact:** We explain the character of God, the depth of human rebellion, and the historical work of Jesus Christ.

- **A Promise of Grace:** We announce that anyone who comes to Christ will find forgiveness, peace with God, and eternal life.

- **A Command to Respond:** The Gospel is not a suggestion; it is a royal decree. God "commands all people everywhere to repent" (Acts 17:30). A call from a King requires a "Yes" or a "No."

The Necessity of the Word

A common mistake in our modern world is thinking we can find our way to God through intuition, nature, or "vague spirituality." While creation tells us that a powerful Creator exists (Chapter 17), only the Word of God reveals that a merciful Savior exists.

This is why the preaching of the Word is so vital. Paul famously asks in Romans 10:14, "How then will they call on him in whom they have not believed? And how are they to believe in him of whom they have never heard? And how are they to hear without someone preaching?" Salvation is a "hearing" event. God has chosen the "folly of what we preach" to be the very vehicle that carries His life-giving call into the hearts of men and women.

Why Do Some Refuse?

The reality of the Gospel call raises a difficult question: if it is such "Good News," why do so many reject it? The Bible tells us that without the Holy Spirit's intervention, our hearts are "hard soil." We are blinded by our own pride, our love for our sin, and the influence of the enemy.

Naming this honestly prevents us from becoming arrogant. When someone responds to the Gospel, it isn't because they are more "spiritually sensitive" or "smarter" than their neighbor. It is because the Grace of God has broken through their defenses. If you find yourself wanting to follow Jesus, it is a sign that God is already at work in you, calling you out of the darkness and into His marvelous light.

Your Responsibility: The Act of Answering

While God is the one who initiates the call and provides the power to respond, we are the ones who must actually answer. God does not believe *for* us; He gives us the grace to believe. The Gospel call is urgent. It is like hearing a knock on the door while the house is on fire; you do not debate the craftsmanship of the door, you open it and run to safety.

The Bible warns, "Today, if you hear his voice, do not harden your hearts" (Hebrews 3:15). Every time we hear the Gospel call and do not respond, our hearts become a little more calloused. But every time we answer the call, we find that the One who called us is also the One who will keep us to the very end.

Weekly Belief Statement

We believe that the Gospel must be sincerely proclaimed to all people as an invitation to salvation in Christ. We affirm that while many hear the external message, it is the Holy Spirit who internally and effectually calls the elect to faith by opening their hearts to the truth. We believe that this call is the necessary means through which God applies the work of redemption to individual lives.

Practical Application

- **Listen for the "Voice within the Voice":** The next time you hear a sermon or read the Bible, don't just listen for information. Ask: "Is the King speaking to my heart right now? What is He asking me to trust or surrender?"

- **Pray for the "Effectual Call":** If you have a friend or family member who hears the Gospel but remains indifferent, pray specifically that God would move from the *external* call to the *internal* call. Ask

Him to "open their heart" as He did for Lydia in the book of Acts.

✟ **Be a Bold Herald:** Since God uses human voices to carry His call, identify one person this week with whom you can share the basic facts of the Gospel. Don't worry about the "results"; your job is simply to deliver the message.

✟ **Check Your "Soil":** Reflect on the Parable of the Sower (Matthew 13). Is your heart currently distracted by "thorns" (worries of this life) or "rocks" (hardened pride)? Ask God to "plow" your heart so His Word can take root.

✟ **Respond with Speed:** If you feel the Holy Spirit prompting you to repent of a specific sin or take a step of faith today, do not wait. Answer the call while the voice is clear.

"Faith comes from hearing, and hearing through the word of Christ." - Romans 10:17

CHAPTER 36
Repent and Believe the Good News

We have arrived at the doorway of the Christian life. In the previous chapter, we heard the "call" of the King. Now, we examine the human response to that call. Throughout the New Testament, when people asked, "What must we do to be saved?" the answer was consistently two-fold: Repent and Believe.

These two actions are often called the "twin graces" or the "two sides of the same coin." You cannot truly have one without the other. To believe in Jesus without repenting of sin is merely an intellectual exercise; to try to repent without believing in Jesus is merely a moral cleanup. Together, they constitute "Conversion", the decisive turn of a human soul from the kingdom of darkness to the Kingdom of God. In this chapter, we will break down what it means to turn *from* and turn *to*, ensuring that our response to the Gospel is as deep as the Gospel itself.

The First Side: Repentance (Turning From)

The word "repentance" has often been misunderstood. Some see it as a feeling of intense guilt or a promise to "never do it again." While emotion and change are involved, the biblical word *metanoia* literally means a "change of mind." It is a fundamental shift in how you view your sin, yourself, and God.

Repentance involves three specific dimensions of the human person:

1. **The Mind (Knowledge):** You recognize that sin is not just a "mistake" but a personal rebellion against a holy God. You agree with God's assessment of your condition.

2. **The Heart (Sorrow):** You experience "godly grief." This is not just being sorry you got caught or sorry you have to face consequences; it is a genuine sorrow that you have offended a loving Creator.

3. **The Will (Action):** You make a conscious decision to forsake sin and head in a new direction. It is an "about-face." As the old hymn says, "I have decided to follow Jesus; no turning back."

True repentance is not just about stopping "bad behaviors." It is about repenting of our "good works" as well, realizing that even our best efforts to save ourselves are "filthy rags" before God. We stop trying to be our own saviors.

The Second Side: Faith (Turning To)

If repentance is the "leaving" of sin, faith is the "clinging" to Christ. Just like repentance, saving faith is more than just a feeling; it is a solid reliance on the Person and work of Jesus. Theologians often describe faith as having three necessary components:

✝ **Notitia (Knowledge):** You must know the facts of the Gospel. You cannot have faith in a Jesus you don't know.

✝ **Assensus (Agreement):** You must believe those facts are true. You agree that Jesus really did die for sins and really did rise from the grave.

✝ **Fiducia (Trust):** This is the "saving" element. It is one thing to believe a chair *can* hold you; it is another thing to actually sit in it. Faith is the act of resting your entire weight on Jesus. It is a personal "Amen" to the promise of God.

Faith is not a "blind leap in the dark." It is a step into the light based on the reliable Word of God. It is the instrument by which we receive everything Jesus accomplished on the Cross.

The Relationship Between the Two

Imagine you are in a burning building. To be saved, you must do two things: you must leave the building (Repentance) and you must climb the ladder provided by the firemen (Faith). If you stay in the building but hold the ladder, you perish. If you leave the building but refuse the ladder, you are still in danger.

In the same way, we turn *away* from our self-reliance and *toward* Christ's sufficiency. This is not a one-time event that happens at the beginning of the Christian life and is then forgotten. Martin Luther famously said that "the entire life of believers should be one of repentance." We never "outgrow" our need to turn from sin and trust in Jesus.

The Source of These Graces

Where do repentance and faith come from? Do we dig them up out of our own willpower? The Bible tells us that both are "gifts of God" (Ephesians 2:8-9; Acts 11:18).

Because we were "dead in our trespasses," we couldn't even want to repent or believe on our own. It is the Holy Spirit who grants us these graces. This is a profound comfort. If you feel even a small desire to turn from your sin and trust in Jesus, that desire is a gift from heaven. You don't have to wait until your repentance is "perfect" or your faith is "strong enough." You simply need to use the gift God is giving you.

The Fruit of Conversion

While we are saved by faith alone, the faith that saves is never alone. It always produces fruit. If someone claims to have "believed the Good News" but their life remains unchanged—if they still love their sin and ignore God's commands—we must ask if they have truly converted.

True repentance leads to a change in life. True faith leads to a life of obedience. We don't do these things to *get* saved, but because we *are* saved. Conversion is the beginning of a life-long journey of becoming who we now are in Christ.

Weekly Belief Statement

We believe that the proper response to the Gospel is repentance toward God and faith in our Lord Jesus Christ. We affirm that saving repentance involves a genuine sorrow for sin and a turning away from it, while saving faith involves a complete and personal trust in the finished work of Christ. We believe that both repentance and faith are gifts of God's grace, produced in the heart by the Holy Spirit.

Practical Application

- **Perform a "Self-Examination":** Look at your life today. Is there a "secret sin" you are coddling rather than repenting of? Name it, agree with God that it is evil, and ask for the grace to turn from it.

- **Practice "The Look":** When you feel the weight of your sin, don't look inward at your own guilt. Look outward at the Cross. Remind yourself: "My faith is not in my goodness, but in His."

- **Identify "Self-Righteousness":** Repentance isn't just for "sinners"; it's for "good people" too. Ask God to show you where you are trusting in your own morality, your church attendance, or your knowledge rather than in Jesus.

✝ **Read the Call to Turn:** Read Ezekiel 33:11 and Mark 1:14-15. Notice the heart of God in these passages—He does not desire the death of the wicked, but that they would turn and live.

✝ **The "Chair" Exercise:** Throughout the day, when you sit in a chair, let it be a physical reminder of faith. Just as you trust the chair to hold you, tell the Lord: "I am resting my soul on You right now."

"The time is fulfilled, and the kingdom of God is at hand; repent and believe in the gospel." - Mark 1:15

CHAPTER 37
Receive New Birth and Union With Christ

If the previous chapters were about the "front porch" of the Christian life, hearing the call and responding in faith, this chapter takes us into the very foundation of our new existence. When a person turns to Christ, something happens that is far more profound than a simple change of mind or a new set of resolutions. A biological miracle occurs in the spiritual realm.

In this chapter, we explore the dual wonders of **Regeneration** (the New Birth) and **Union with Christ.** We will see that salvation is not just a legal transaction where your debts are paid; it is an organic transformation where you are given a new life and fused to a new Source. This is the "how" behind the Christian's ability to change: we don't just follow Jesus; we are *in* Jesus, and His life now pulses through our veins.

The Mystery of the New Birth

When a high-ranking religious leader named Nicodemus came to Jesus under the cover of night, he expected a theological debate. Instead, Jesus told him something radical: "Unless one is born again he cannot see the kingdom of God" (John 3:3).

Regeneration is a work of the Holy Spirit where He imparts spiritual life to a soul that was previously "dead in trespasses and sins" (Chapter 25). Just as you did not contribute to your physical birth, you do not contribute to your spiritual birth. It is an act of "monergism", a fancy way of saying God does the work alone.

> ✝ **The Heart Transplant:** The prophet Ezekiel described it as God removing a "heart of stone" and replacing it with a "heart of flesh" (Ezekiel 36:26).

✝ **The Result:** Suddenly, things you once found boring (like Scripture) become beautiful. Things you once loved (like sin) become repulsive. The New Birth changes your "want-to."

Union with Christ: The Spiritual Fusion

The New Birth is the start, but **Union with Christ** is the status. This is arguably the most important phrase in the New Testament. The writers use the phrase "in Christ" or "in Him" over 200 times.

Union with Christ means that, by the power of the Spirit, the believer is spiritually bound to Jesus. Everything that is true of Him becomes true of you. Because He was crucified, you are "crucified with Christ." Because He was raised, you are "raised with Him." Because He is the beloved Son, you are a "beloved child."

Think of it like a branch grafted into a vine. The branch doesn't have its own life; it draws its life, its strength, and its ability to produce fruit entirely from the vine. Apart from the vine, the branch can do nothing. In Christ, you have access to all the "sap" of the Spirit.

The Legal and Vital Connection

Our union with Christ functions in two distinct but inseparable ways:

1. **The Legal Union:** Because we are "in Christ," He acts as our representative. In the courtroom of God, when the Judge looks at us, He sees the record of Jesus. Our union ensures that His "Active Obedience" (Chapter 30) and His "Saving Work" (Chapter 31) are credited to us.

2. **The Vital Union:** This is the "pulse" of our daily lives. Because we are "in Christ," His Spirit dwells in us. We aren't just forgiven for the past; we are empowered for the present. His strength becomes our strength in temptation; His peace becomes our peace in turmoil.

The New Identity

One of the greatest struggles in a broken world is the search for identity. We try to find our value in our jobs, our looks, our social standing, or our successes. But if you are born again and united to Christ, your identity is "hidden with Christ in God" (Colossians 3:3).

This identity is **unshakable**. If you lose your job, you are still "in Christ." If your health fails, you are still "in Christ." If people reject you, you are still "in Christ." Your core reality is no longer defined by your performance or your failures, but by your connection to the King of the Universe. This is the secret to a life of "holy confidence."

Living from the Union

Many Christians live as if they are "outside" Christ, trying to work their way back in. They think they need to "do better" so God will be close to them. But the doctrine of Union tells us the opposite: God is close to you because you are in His Son.

We don't work *for* a relationship with God; we work *from* the relationship we already have. When we fight sin, we aren't fighting to "get saved"; we are fighting because we *are* saved image-bearers of the King. When we pray, we aren't shouting into the void; we are speaking from within the very heart of the Son to the Father.

Weekly Belief Statement

We believe that salvation involves a supernatural work of regeneration by the Holy Spirit, whereby we are born again and given a new heart. We affirm that every believer is spiritually united to Jesus Christ in a vital and legal union. We believe that being "in Christ" means we share in His death, resurrection, and life, and that our identity and power for living are found solely in Him.

Practical Application

- ✝ **The "In Christ" Meditation:** Every morning this week, before you look at your phone, say to yourself: "I am in Christ. Everything true of Him is credited to me." Notice how this changes your stress levels.

- ✝ **Identify "Branch Behavior":** When you feel exhausted or "dried up" spiritually, ask yourself: "Am I trying to produce fruit on my own, or am I resting in the Vine?" Spend ten minutes in silent prayer, "re-attaching" your heart to Jesus.

- ✝ **Read the High Priestly Prayer:** Read John 17. Pay close attention to how Jesus prays for us to be "one" with Him as He is with the Father. Realize that your union was the desire of Jesus' heart before He went to the Cross.

- ✝ **Audit Your Identity:** List the three things you usually use to define your worth (e.g., career, parenting, fitness). For each one, pray: "Lord, help me see that even if I lose this, I am still secure in You."

✞ **Walk in Newness:** If you are struggling with a persistent sin, stop saying "I'm just a sinner." Start saying, "I am a new creation in Christ. That sin does not belong to who I am anymore." Act on the truth of your new birth.

"Therefore, if anyone is in Christ, he is a new creation.
The old has passed away; behold, the new has come." -
2 Corinthians 5:17

CHAPTER 38
Stand Justified by Faith

We have reached the "legal heart" of the Christian life. If regeneration (Chapter 37) is about our **nature** being changed, justification is about our **status** being changed. Imagine standing in the highest courtroom in the universe, facing a Judge who knows every secret thought and every hidden motive you've ever had. The evidence against you is undeniable. The law is perfect. The sentence is just. And yet, the Judge brings down the gavel and declares: *"Not Guilty. In fact—Righteous."*

This is the miracle of **Justification**. It is the breathtaking reality that, through faith in Christ, God looks at you as if you had never sinned and as if you had always obeyed. In this chapter, we will explore why this "forensic" (legal) declaration is the only foundation for true peace. We will look at how we are justified, why it is by faith alone, and how this verdict changes the way you look at yourself, your past, and your future.

The Divine Courtroom: Understanding the Verdict

In our modern world, we often think of salvation in therapeutic terms— God "healing" us or making us "feel better." While God certainly does those things, the Bible primary uses the language of the courtroom to describe our standing before Him. Justification is a **forensic term**. It doesn't mean God "makes us good" in this moment (that is sanctification, which we will cover next); it means He "declares us righteous."

To be justified is the opposite of being condemned. When a judge condemns someone, he isn't making them a bad person; he is declaring that they *are* a lawbreaker in the eyes of the state. Conversely, when God justifies you, He is declaring that you are a law-keeper in His eyes. He doesn't look at your record of failure; He looks at the record of His Son.

The Mechanism of Grace: Imputation

How can a holy and just God declare a sinner to be righteous without lying or being corrupt? The answer lies in a concept we've touched on before: **Imputation**.

There are three great "imputations" in the Bible:

1. **Adam's sin was imputed to us:** We inherited his fallen status.
2. **Our sin was imputed to Christ:** On the Cross, our "debt" was placed on His account, and He paid it.
3. **Christ's righteousness is imputed to us:** His perfect "credit" is placed on our account.

This is the "Great Exchange." In justification, God does not wait for you to actually *be* perfect before He accepts you. Instead, He "clothes" you in the perfect life of Jesus. You are standing before God wearing the "moral resume" of the King of Kings. This is why you can have confidence even on your worst days—because your standing with God is based on Christ's performance, not your own.

Faith: The Empty Hand of the Beggar

If justification is the gift, faith is the hand that receives it. The Reformers famously used the Latin phrase **Sola Fide**, Faith Alone. This means that we do not contribute anything to our justification. We don't bring our good works, our religious rituals, or our "decent behavior" to the table.

Faith is not a "work" that we do to earn God's favor. Rather, faith is the "instrument" of justification. Think of it like a beggar receiving a million-dollar check. The beggar didn't earn the money by reaching out his hand; the money was a gift. The hand was simply the means of receiving it. In the same way, faith is our way of saying, "I have nothing to offer, Lord. I trust only in Jesus."

> "Faith is a living, daring confidence in God's grace, so sure and certain that a man would stake his life on it a thousand times." — *Martin Luther*

Justification vs. Sanctification: Why the Distinction Matters

It is vital to distinguish between these two "S-words." If we confuse them, we lose the Gospel.

Justification	Sanctification
Happens **outside** of us (a legal declaration).	Happens **inside** of us (a moral transformation).
Happens **instantly** the moment we believe.	Happens **gradually** over the course of a lifetime.

| Is **perfect** and complete from day one. | Is **imperfect** and ongoing until we die. |
| Is the **ground** of our peace with God. | Is the **fruit** of our peace with God. |

If you think your justification depends on your sanctification (how much you are growing), you will live in constant anxiety. You will always wonder if you have done "enough" to be accepted. But when you realize that your justification is a finished legal fact, you are finally free to grow in sanctification out of love, not fear.

The Results of the Verdict: Peace and Access

The immediate result of being justified is stated clearly in Romans 5:1: "Therefore, since we have been justified by faith, we have **peace with God** through our Lord Jesus Christ."

This isn't just a "feeling" of peace; it is the objective end of the war. Because the legal case against you is closed, there is no more enmity between you and your Creator. You are no longer an "enemy" or even just a "subject"; you are a "friend" and an "heir."

Furthermore, justification gives us **permanent access**. We don't have to wait for a special day or a special mood to talk to God. Because we are "in Christ," the door to the Father's presence is always standing wide open. You can come to Him in your weakness, in your failure, and in your joy, knowing that He sees you through the lens of His Son's perfection.

Common Misunderstandings: "Faith without Works?"

When people hear about justification by faith alone, a common objection arises: "Does this mean I can just live however I want?" The Apostle Paul anticipated this and gave a resounding "By no means!" (Romans 6:1).

While we are justified by faith *alone*, the faith that justifies is never *alone*. If you truly trust in Jesus, you will want to follow Him. If you truly believe you have been saved from a burning building, you won't try to run back inside. Good works are not the **cause** of our justification, but they are the inevitable **evidence** of it. As the book of James reminds us, a "faith" that produces no change in life is not saving faith at all—it's just an intellectual opinion.

The Assurance of the Verdict

One of the most beautiful things about justification is that it is **irrevocable**. In a human court, a verdict might be overturned on appeal. But in God's court, there is no higher authority. Romans 8:33–34 asks the triumphant question: "Who shall bring any charge against God's elect? It is God who justifies. Who is to condemn?"

If God has declared you righteous, no demon in hell and no accuser on earth can change that status. Even your own conscience, when it tries to condemn you, must bow to the verdict of the Judge. You are safe. You are secure. You are justified.

Weekly Belief Statement

We believe that justification is an act of God's free grace, wherein He pardons all our sins and accepts us as righteous in His sight. We affirm that this is not based on anything wrought in us or done by us, but only on the perfect obedience and full satisfaction of Christ, imputed to us and received by faith alone. We believe that this verdict brings objective peace with God and serves as the only foundation for a life of true holiness.

Practical Application

- ✝ **Silence the Accuser:** This week, when you feel a sense of "vague guilt" or the "whispers of condemnation," stop and speak the truth to yourself. Say: *"It is God who justifies. Who is to condemn? I am righteous in Christ."*

- ✝ **The "Empty Hand" Prayer:** When you go to God in prayer this week, resist the urge to start by telling Him how "good" you've been. Instead, start by acknowledging your need. Say: *"Lord, I come with empty hands, resting only on what Jesus did."*

- ✝ **Audit Your "Peace Level":** If you are living in constant fear of God's displeasure, you might be confusing justification and sanctification. Spend 15 minutes reading Romans 8:1-4 and ask the Holy Spirit to help you rest in the "No Condemnation" reality.

- ✝ **Observe Your Motivation:** Notice *why* you are doing good things this week (like helping a neighbor or reading your Bible). Are you doing it to "get" God to like you, or because you already know He loves you in Christ?

✝ **Study the "Exchange":** Read 2 Corinthians 5:21 and write it on a post-it note. Place it somewhere you will see it daily to remind yourself of the "Great Exchange" that defines your life.

"For our sake he made him to be sin who knew no sin, so that in him we might become the righteousness of God." -
2 Corinthians 5:21

CHAPTER 39
Grow in Sanctification Day by Day

If justification is the "title deed" that says you own the house, **sanctification** is the lifelong process of actually moving in, cleaning out the cobwebs, repairing the broken windows, and remodeling the interior to reflect the character of the Owner. In our previous chapter, we marveled at the legal reality that we are declared perfectly righteous in God's sight the moment we believe. But any honest Christian knows that while our *standing* is perfect, our *state* is still under construction. We are "saints" who still struggle with "sin."

This chapter explores the messy, beautiful, and essential work of growing in holiness. Sanctification is the process by which the Holy Spirit works in us to conform our character to the image of Jesus Christ. It is not a way to "stay" saved, but a result of "being" saved. It is the evidence of the new life we received in regeneration. To grow in sanctification day by day is to participate in the most significant transformation a human being can experience: the slow death of the old self and the steady rising of the new.

Positional vs. Progressive Holiness

To understand sanctification, we must first distinguish between its two "modes." Without this distinction, you will either become a legalist (trying to earn God's love) or a defeatist (giving up because you aren't perfect yet).

✝ **Positional Sanctification:** The moment you are united to Christ, you are "set apart" for God. In this sense, every believer is already "holy." This is why the Apostle Paul addresses the messy, struggling Christians in Corinth as "saints." Your identity is fixed. You belong to God.

✝ **Progressive Sanctification:** This is the day-to-day reality of becoming in practice what you already are in position. It is the "becoming" part. It is a process that begins at conversion and is only completed when we see Jesus face-to-face (Glorification).

While justification is a "point" event, sanctification is a "line" event. It takes time. It involves growth, setbacks, and perseverance. It is the "long obedience in the same direction."

The Miracle of Synergism: Who Does the Work?

One of the most unique aspects of sanctification is its nature as a **synergistic** work. In regeneration (the New Birth), God works alone—you were spiritually dead and He gave you life. But in sanctification, God works, and *you* work because He is working in you.

The classic text for this is Philippians 2:12-13: *"Work out your own salvation with fear and trembling, for it is God who works in you, both to will and to work for his good pleasure."*

Notice the tension:

1. **Our Responsibility:** "Work out your own salvation." We are called to effort. We are called to fight, to run, to pray, and to resist.

2. **God's Enablement:** "For it is God who works in you." We only have the "will" and the "power" to change because the Holy Spirit is fueling us.

We are not "passive" in our growth. We don't just "let go and let God." Instead, we "act the miracle." We put forth effort, but we do so while leaning entirely on the grace of the Spirit. If you try to work without God, you get legalism; if you try to let God work without your participation, you get stagnation.

The Two Movements: Mortification and Vivification

Sanctification is not just about "adding" good habits; it's about a radical internal reshuffling. Traditionally, this has been described through two movements: **Mortification** and **Vivification.**

1. Mortification (The Killing of Sin)

The Apostle Paul tells us to "put to death" the deeds of the body. Mortification is the active, aggressive rejection of sin. It is not just "managing" your temper or "avoiding" certain websites; it is a heart-level war against the "flesh."

- It involves identifying the "roots" of sin (like pride or fear) rather than just the "fruits."

- It requires "starving" the old nature by removing the triggers and temptations that lead us astray.

✝ As John Owen famously said: *"Be killing sin or it will be killing you."*

2. Vivification (The Making Alive)

We don't just clear out the weeds; we plant the garden. Vivification is the process of being "made alive" to righteousness. It is the cultivation of the "Fruit of the Spirit", love, joy, peace, patience, and the rest.

✝ It is the "renewal of the mind" where we begin to love what God loves and hate what God hates.

✝ It is the "putting on" of Christ, where His reactions and His priorities become our own.

The "Tools" of Growth: The Means of Grace

God does not leave us to grow in a vacuum. He has provided specific "instruments" or "means of grace" through which the Holy Spirit normally works to change us. While these activities don't "earn" us holiness, they position us to receive the Spirit's transforming power.

✝ **The Word of God:** Jesus prayed, "Sanctify them in the truth; your word is truth." The Bible is the mirror that shows us our sin and the map that shows us the Savior. We do not just read it; we let it read us.

✝ **Prayer:** This is the "breathing" of the soul. Through prayer, we acknowledge our dependence on God and align our wills with His. It is the primary way we "draw sap" from the Vine (Chapter 37).

✝ **The Community of Faith:** Sanctification is a team sport. We need the "one anothers" of the Church, to be encouraged, rebuked, and spurred on toward love and good deeds. You cannot grow into Christlikeness in isolation.

✝ **Suffering and Trials:** As we saw in Chapter 21, God often uses the "fire" of difficulty to refine our faith. Trials strip away our self-reliance and force us to cling more tightly to Christ.

The Zig-Zag of Progress

If you expected sanctification to be a straight diagonal line toward perfection, you will quickly become discouraged. For most of us, growth looks like "two steps forward, one step back."

There will be seasons of rapid growth where victory feels easy, and seasons of "spiritual desert" where every inch of progress feels like a battle. The key is not the speed of the progress, but the **direction** of the life. Are you more aware of your sin than you were five years ago? Do you find yourself running to Christ more quickly when you fail? Are you more patient with others because you realize how patient God has been with you? These are the real signs of sanctification.

The Goal: Conformed to the Image of the Son

What is the "end product" of sanctification? It is not just being a "nice person" or a "moral citizen." The goal is that we would be **conformed to the image of His Son** (Romans 8:29).

God is making you look like Jesus. He is working to give you the heart of Christ, the mind of Christ, and the hands of Christ. This is why our focus in sanctification must always stay on Jesus. We don't become holy by staring at our own progress; we become holy by "beholding the glory of the Lord" (2 Corinthians 3:18). As we gaze at Him, we are transformed into His likeness "from one degree of glory to another."

Weekly Belief Statement

We believe that sanctification is the work of God's free grace, whereby we are renewed in the whole man after the image of God and are enabled more and more to die unto sin and live unto righteousness. We affirm that while this work is imperfect in this life, it is a necessary fruit of our union with Christ. We commit to using the means of grace and putting forth diligent effort to grow in holiness, trusting in the Spirit's power to complete the work He has begun.

Practical Application

- **Identify One "Mortification" Target:** What is the one sin or habit that most consistently trips you up? This week, don't just "try harder." Identify the *root* (e.g., "I lie because I fear people's opinions") and create a specific plan to starve that sin (e.g., "I will confess this to a friend and invite accountability").

- **Pick One "Vivification" Goal:** Choose one "Fruit of the Spirit" (like patience or gentleness) that you currently lack. Pray specifically every morning: "Holy Spirit, produce *Your* patience in me today in my interactions with my coworkers."

✝ **Use the "Mirror" Daily:** Spend 15 minutes each morning in the Word. Don't look for a "life hack"; look for a glimpse of God's character. Ask: "How does this passage show me the beauty of Jesus?"

✝ **Practice "Immediate Repentance":** When you fail this week (and you will), do not wallow in guilt for hours. Immediately acknowledge it, claim your justification in Christ, and ask for the strength to get back on the path.

✝ **Invite an "Iron-Sharpener":** Ask a trusted Christian friend, "In what area do you see me growing, and in what area do you think I need to be more watchful?" Listen with humility and without defensiveness.

"It is God's will that you should be sanctified: that you should avoid sexual immorality." - 1 Thessalonians 4:3

CHAPTER 40
Hold Fast With Assurance and Perseverance

If you have ever been on a long-distance flight through heavy turbulence, you know the difference between being "safe" and "feeling safe." Objectively, you are in a multi-ton machine designed to withstand incredible stress; subjectively, your knuckles are white and your heart is racing. The Christian life often feels like that flight. We have discussed the legal reality of justification and the internal miracle of the new birth, but as the journey continues and the "turbulence" of doubt, sin, and suffering hits, the question inevitably arises: *Can I lose this? Will I make it to the end?*

This chapter addresses the twin pillars of the believer's security: **The Perseverance of the Saints** (the objective reality that God keeps His own) and **The Assurance of Salvation** (the subjective confidence that you are, indeed, one of His). To "hold fast" is not an act of desperate strength on our part, but a response to the fact that we are being held by an Almighty hand.

1. The Divine Grip: The Perseverance of the Saints

The phrase "Perseverance of the Saints" is a bit of a misnomer. It might be better described as the "Preservation of the Savior." While the Bible certainly calls us to persevere, the only reason we *can* persevere is that God is preserving us. This doctrine is the logical conclusion of everything we have studied in Part 7. If salvation is a work of God from start to finish—if He called you, regenerated you, and justified you, then He is responsible for completing that work.

The Apostle Paul famously outlines this in what theologians call "The Golden Chain of Salvation" in Romans 8:

> *"For those whom he foreknew he also predestined to be conformed to the image of his Son... And those whom he predestined he also called, and those whom he called he*

Notice that the chain is unbroken. There is no "leakage" between being justified and being glorified. If you are in the first link, you will be in the last. This is because the ground of our security is not the strength of our faith, but the faithfulness of our God. Jesus Himself promised:

*"I give them eternal life, and they will never perish, and
no one will snatch them out of my hand" (John 10:28).*

2. The Quest for Certainty: What is Assurance?

If Perseverance is the "fact" of our security, Assurance is the "feeling" of it. It is possible to be a true Christian and struggle with assurance (feeling like you aren't saved), just as it is possible to be a false convert and have a false sense of assurance (feeling like you are saved when you aren't).

Assurance is a gift, but it is also something that can grow or diminish based on our walk with Christ. It is not an "optional extra" for the super-spiritual; it is the "oil" in the engine of the Christian life. Without it, you will serve God out of a place of fear and insecurity; with it, you serve out of a place of gratitude and joy.

So, how do we know? Theologians often speak of the "three-legged stool" of assurance. If one leg is missing, the stool falls over.

The First Leg: The Promises of the Word

Our assurance must begin with the objective Word of God. We don't look into our hearts first; we look at the Cross. 1 John 5:13 says, *"I write these things to you who believe in the name of the Son of God, that you may **know** that you have eternal life."* If God says that everyone who believes in the Son has life, and you know you are resting in the Son, then you have life. This is the "logic of faith."

The Second Leg: The Inward Witness of the Spirit

The Holy Spirit doesn't just change us; He talks to us. Romans 8:16 tells us, *"The Spirit himself bears witness with our spirit that we are children of God."* This is often an intuitive, deep-seated sense of peace or a sudden realization of God's Fatherly love. It is the "Amen" in our souls when we read the promises of Scripture.

The Third Leg: The Evidence of a Changed Life

As we saw in Chapter 39 (Sanctification), the New Birth produces fruit. While we aren't saved *by* our works, we are assured *by* our works. If you find that you now hate the sin you once loved, if you love the people of

God, and if you have a desire to obey the King, those are "spiritual vital signs." They prove that there is life in the body.

3. The Problem of Apostasy: Why Do Some Fall Away?

One of the most difficult questions in the "Map of Reality" is why some people who seemed to be vibrant Christians eventually walk away, deny the faith, or return to a life of blatant sin. This is called **Apostasy**.

The doctrine of Perseverance does not claim that everyone who *says* they are a Christian will make it to heaven. It claims that everyone who *is* a Christian will make it to heaven. The Apostle John explains the phenomenon of people leaving the church this way:

"They went out from us, but they were not of us; for if they had been of us, they would have continued with us"
(1 John 2:19).

Apostasy is not a person "losing" their salvation; it is a person revealing that, despite their outward appearance, they never had the internal miracle of regeneration. They had the "external call" (Chapter 35) but not the "internal change." This should not make us paranoid, but it should make us sober and diligent.

4. The Warnings of Scripture: Threats or Tools?

If our security is guaranteed by God, why does the Bible contain so many warnings? (e.g., "If you do not remain in me, you are thrown away like a branch").

Think of a sign on a winding mountain road that says, *"Warning: Sharp Curve. 1000-foot drop."* Does the government put that sign there because they *want* you to fall off the cliff? No, they put it there to *keep* you on the road. The warnings of Scripture are the "guardrails" God uses to keep His children from wandering off into destruction. A true child of God hears the warning, feels a healthy "fear of the Lord," and stays on the path. The warning is the very means God uses to ensure our perseverance.

5. Wrestling with Doubt

What about the believer who truly loves God but is haunted by the fear that they aren't "in"? Doubt is a normal part of the Christian experience, often caused by:

> ✝ **Unconfessed Sin:** Sin clouds our vision and makes God feel distant.

> ✝ **Physical Exhaustion:** Sometimes we don't need a sermon; we need a nap and a meal.

✝ **Spiritual Attack:** The "accuser" (Chapter 31) loves to tell us we don't belong to the King.

✝ **Misunderstanding Grace:** Thinking that our standing with God depends on our daily performance rather than Christ's.

In these seasons, the strategy is not to "try harder" to feel saved. The strategy is to "look away" from yourself. As Robert Murray M'Cheyne famously said, *"For every look at yourself, take ten looks at Christ."* You don't get assurance by measuring the strength of your grip on Him; you get it by realizing the strength of His grip on you.

6. The "Heed" and the "Hope"

Holding fast is a combination of **vigilance** and **confidence**. We are vigilant because the journey is dangerous and our hearts are prone to wander. We are confident because our Captain has already reached the shore and has promised to bring us there too.

Perseverance is not a "license to sin." If someone says, "I'm saved, so I can live like the devil," they are proving they don't understand the Gospel. True assurance leads to deeper holiness. The more you realize how secure you are in the Father's love, the more you want to please Him. Security is the "fuel" of the Christian life, not the "finish line."

7. The Final Glorification

The ultimate end of our perseverance is **Glorification**. This is the final step in the Map of Reality, where we are finally and fully freed from the presence of sin, given resurrected bodies, and welcomed into the visible presence of the King. The reason we hold fast today is that we know what is waiting for us tomorrow.

Perseverance is the "waiting room" for glory. It is the grit and the grace that carries us through the "middle" of the story until we reach the "happily ever after" that God has prepared for those who love Him.

Weekly Belief Statement

We believe that all those who are truly born again and united to Christ will never finally fall away from the state of grace, but shall certainly persevere to the end and be eternally saved. We affirm that this perseverance is not based on human merit or willpower, but on the unchangeable decree of God, the efficacy of Christ's intercession, and the abiding presence of the Holy Spirit. We believe that a personal assurance of salvation is a possible and desirable blessing for every believer.

Practical Application

✞ **Audit Your Assurance:** Using the "three-legged stool," ask yourself:

1. Am I resting in the promises of the Word?
2. Am I seeing the fruit of a changed heart?
3. Am I experiencing the Spirit's witness? Thank God for the legs that are strong and ask for help where you feel shaky.

✞ **Memorize a "Security Text":** When doubt hits, you need a weapon. Memorize John 10:27-29 or Romans 8:38-39. Recite it aloud when you feel the "turbulence" of doubt.

✞ **Practice "Gospel Reminding":** Every morning this week, tell yourself: *"My standing with God today is not based on how well I persevere for Him, but on how perfectly Jesus persevered for me."*

✞ **Check the Guardrails:** Are there any "warning signs" in Scripture that you have been ignoring? (e.g., warnings about greed, anger, or pride). Repent of those areas today, thanking God that His warnings are a sign of His Fatherly care.

✞ **Encourage a "Doubting Thomas":** Reach out to a friend who is going through a hard time or struggling with their faith. Remind them of the "Divine Grip" and share a verse that has given you confidence in the past.

"And I am sure of this, that he who began a good work in you will bring it to completion at the day of Jesus Christ."
- Philippians 1:6

CHAPTER 41
Walk by the Spirit and Bear Fruit

We have established that the Christian life is a "new life" (Chapter 37) and that we are called to grow in holiness every day (Chapter 39). But how does this actually happen on a Tuesday afternoon when you're stuck in traffic, or during a heated argument with a spouse, or in the quiet moments when old temptations whisper in your ear? If the Christian life were merely a set of rules to follow, we would all eventually collapse under the weight of our own inadequacy.

The secret to the "Map of Reality" is that the Christian life is not a solo performance; it is a **Spirit-empowered walk.** In this chapter, we explore the vital command to "walk by the Spirit" and the beautiful "fruit" that inevitably grows when we do. We will look at the internal conflict between our old nature and the Spirit, the specific character traits that define a person in-dwelt by God, and the practical rhythm of "keeping in step" with the Third Person of the Trinity.

1. The Command: What Does it Mean to "Walk"?

In Galatians 5:16, the Apostle Paul gives a simple but profound instruction:

> *"Walk by the Spirit, and you will not gratify the desires of the flesh."*

The metaphor of "walking" is intentionally ordinary. It's not a sprint, which implies a short burst of energy. It's not a leap, which implies a miraculous jump over problems. A walk is a steady, step-by-step, repetitive motion that takes you from where you are to where you are going.

- ✝ **Walking implies progress:** You aren't standing still; you are moving toward Christlikeness.

- ✝ **Walking implies dependence:** To walk with someone, you must stay near them, listen to them, and move at their pace.

✝ **Walking implies a destination:** We are walking toward our final glorification.

To walk by the Spirit means to live in a state of constant, moment-by-moment reliance on the Holy Spirit's presence and power. It is the practice of "drawing breath" from the Spirit before we speak, act, or react.

2. The Civil War: Spirit vs. Flesh

The moment you are born again, a "civil war" begins within your soul. Before Christ, you had only one nature: the "Flesh" (the fallen human nature prone to self-centeredness and sin). Now, you have the Holy Spirit dwelling within you. These two are in total opposition.

Paul describes this tension vividly:

"For the desires of the flesh are against the Spirit, and the desires of the Spirit are against the flesh, for these are opposed to each other" (Galatians 5:17).

It is important to understand that the presence of this conflict is not a sign that you aren't a Christian; it is a sign that you **are**. A dead person doesn't fight; only a living person struggles. The "Flesh" wants to be the king of its own island, while the Spirit wants to glorify Jesus. Walking by the Spirit doesn't mean the Flesh disappears; it means the Spirit is given the steering wheel so the Flesh is no longer in control.

3. The Works vs. The Fruit

To help us identify who is winning the war in any given moment, the Bible provides two lists. One is a list of "works" (manufactured by human effort and sin), and the other is a list of "fruit" (grown organically by the Spirit).

The Works of the Flesh (Self-Life)	The Fruit of the Spirit (Christ-Life)
Sexual immorality, impurity, sensuality	**Love, Joy, Peace**
Idolatry, sorcery, enmity, strife	**Patience, Kindness, Goodness**
Jealousy, fits of anger, rivalries	**Faithfulness, Gentleness**
Dissensions, divisions, envy, drunkenness	**Self-Control**

Notice the linguistic difference: **Works** are plural, noisy, and often forced. **Fruit** is singular. While there are nine traits listed, they are all part of one "cluster." You cannot truly have Spirit-led "Joy" without also having Spirit-led "Kindness." The Fruit of the Spirit is essentially a portrait of the character of Jesus Christ.

4. A Deep Dive into the Fruit

Let's examine this "cluster" more closely. These are not personality traits you are born with; they are supernatural qualities the Spirit produces in you.

✝ **Love (Agape):** Not a fickle feeling, but a sacrificial commitment to the well-being of others, even our enemies. It is the "root" of all other fruit.

✝ **Joy:** A deep-seated confidence in God's sovereignty that remains even when circumstances are painful. It is the "cheerfulness" of the soul in God.

✝ **Peace (Shalom):** A tranquility of heart that comes from knowing our "legal status" with God (Justification) is secure.

✝ **Patience (Long-suffering):** The ability to endure difficult people or circumstances without lashing out or giving up.

✝ **Kindness & Goodness:** Kindness is the *disposition* of being helpful; Goodness is that disposition in *action*. It is being "generous in spirit."

✝ **Faithfulness:** Being reliable, trustworthy, and loyal to God and others over the long haul.

✝ **Gentleness:** Often mistaken for weakness, gentleness is actually "power under control." It is the way Jesus handled the bruised reed and the smoldering wick.

✝ **Self-Control:** The irony of the Spirit's work. He empowers *you* to govern *your* desires. It is the ability to say "no" to the Flesh so you can say "yes" to God.

5. How to Cultivate the Fruit

You cannot "will" a piece of fruit into existence. A branch doesn't strain and groan to produce an apple; it simply stays attached to the tree and receives the nutrients. This brings us back to Jesus' teaching in John 15:

"Abide in me, and I in you. As the branch cannot bear fruit by itself, unless it abides in the vine, neither can you, unless you abide in me."

Cultivating the fruit is about **Abiding**.

✝ **Abiding through the Word:** Letting God's truth saturate your thinking so you begin to see the world as He does.

✝ **Abiding through Prayer:** Continually turning your gaze toward Christ throughout the day.

✝ **Abiding through Obedience:** When the Spirit prompts you to do something, you do it. Each act of obedience is a "step" in the walk.

6. Keeping in Step: The Rhythm of Grace

In Galatians 5:25, Paul adds a subtle nuance:

*"If we live by the Spirit, let us also **keep in step** with the Spirit."*

The Greek word for "keep in step" (*stoicheō*) refers to soldiers marching in a straight line. It implies a rhythm. The Holy Spirit is moving; our job is to stay in sync with Him.

✝ If the Spirit is moving toward a person in need, and you are moving toward your own comfort, you are out of step.

✝ If the Spirit is prompting you to be quiet and listen, but you are rushing to defend yourself, you are out of step.

"Keeping in step" requires a quiet heart. You cannot hear the "gentle whisper" of the Spirit if your life is filled with the constant "white noise" of digital distraction, busyness, and self-promotion. Walking by the Spirit requires a deliberate slowing down to notice His leadings.

7. The Result: A Life of Freedom

The chapter on the Spirit and the Flesh ends with a fascinating phrase:

"Against such things there is no law" (Galatians 5:23).

This is the ultimate goal of the "Map of Reality." When you are walking by the Spirit and bearing His fruit, you don't need a list of "Thou Shalt Nots" to keep you in line. Why? Because the Spirit has changed your desires. If you are filled with Love, you don't need a law telling you not to murder. If you are filled with Self-Control, you don't need a law telling you not to be a drunkard.

Walking by the Spirit is the transition from **external regulation** (The Law) to **internal transformation** (Grace). It is the life of a son or daughter who wants to please their Father, rather than a slave who is afraid of the whip. It is the most beautiful, free, and adventurous way to live.

Weekly Belief Statement

We believe that the Holy Spirit dwells within every believer, providing the power to overcome the desires of the flesh and to live a life pleasing to God. We affirm that as we abide in Christ and walk by the Spirit, He produces in us the fruit of love, joy, peace, patience, kindness, goodness, faithfulness, gentleness, and self-control. We believe that this Spirit-led life is the only way to fulfill the moral requirements of God and to reflect the character of Jesus to the world.

Practical Application

- **The "Morning Submission":** Before you get out of bed, pray a simple prayer: *"Holy Spirit, I surrender the 'steering wheel' of my life to You today. Help me to walk in step with You and notice Your prompts."*

- **The "Fruit Check":** Pick one specific fruit (e.g., Gentleness) and focus on it for 24 hours. Every time you are about to speak, ask: *"Is this word coming from my Flesh or from the Spirit's Gentleness?"*

- **Identify the "Clutter":** What is the "noise" in your life that prevents you from hearing the Spirit? Choose one thing to fast from this week (social media, podcasts, etc.) to create space for "keeping in step."

- **Read the Contrast:** Read Galatians 5:16–26 every day this week. Pay attention to the "Works of the Flesh" and ask God to show you which ones are currently "weeds" in your heart's garden.

- **Practice "The Pivot":** When you feel a "fit of anger" or "jealousy" rising (Works of the Flesh), don't just suppress it. "Pivot" to the Spirit. Say: *"Lord, I am feeling the Flesh right now. I choose to rest in Your Peace instead."*

"But the fruit of the Spirit is love, joy, peace, patience, kindness, goodness, faithfulness, gentleness, self-control; against such things there is no law." - Galatians 5:22–23

CHAPTER 42
Pray, Fight Sin, and Grow Strong

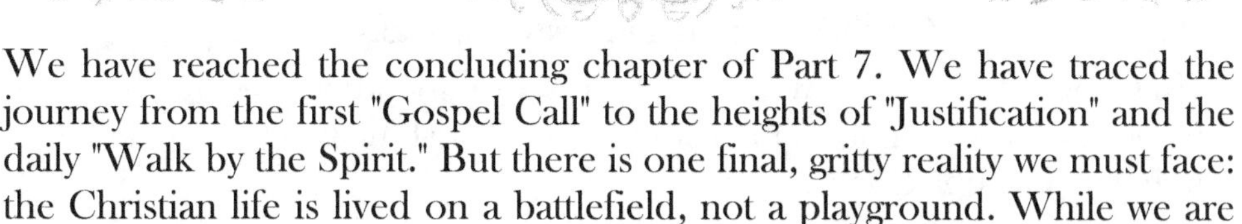

We have reached the concluding chapter of Part 7. We have traced the journey from the first "Gospel Call" to the heights of "Justification" and the daily "Walk by the Spirit." But there is one final, gritty reality we must face: the Christian life is lived on a battlefield, not a playground. While we are securely "in Christ," we remain in a world that is still under the influence of the Fall, carrying a "flesh" that is prone to wander, and facing an enemy who is "like a roaring lion, seeking someone to devour" (1 Peter 5:8).

If you try to live this new life on autopilot, you will soon find yourself exhausted and discouraged. To "Receive Salvation and Walk in New Life" requires a tactical mindset. In this chapter, we explore the three essential habits of the resilient believer: **persistent prayer, the active fight against sin, and the intentional cultivation of spiritual strength.** This is where the theology of the previous chapters meets the "mud and blood" of daily existence.

1. Prayer: Communication for Combat

Many people view prayer as a spiritual "suggestion box" or a way to get God to approve their personal grocery list of desires. But in the Map of Reality, prayer is more like a wartime radio. It is the vital link between the soldier on the ground and the Commander at headquarters.

The Nature of Prayer

Prayer is the primary way we "abide" in the Vine (Chapter 37). It is the acknowledgement of our utter dependence. When we stop praying, we are essentially saying, "I've got this on my own." And that is exactly when we become most vulnerable.

✝ **Prayer as Intimacy:** It is the conversation between a child and a Father. It involves adoration, confession, and thanksgiving.

✝ **Prayer as Petition:** It is asking God to intervene in our lives and the lives of others.

✝ **Prayer as Intercession:** It is standing in the gap for a broken world, pleading for the King's justice and mercy to be manifest.

Why Prayer Feels Hard

If prayer is so important, why is it often the first thing we neglect? Because it is an act of war. The "Flesh" hates prayer because prayer is the death of self-reliance. The Enemy hates prayer because it activates the power of Heaven. To pray, then, is to choose to be "strong in the Lord" rather than strong in yourself.

2. The Art of Mortification: Fighting Sin Tactically

In Chapter 39, we discussed "Mortification" (the killing of sin). Now, we look at the *how*. You do not kill sin by simply wishing it away; you kill it by starving it and replacing it.

Identifying the "Gateway" Sins

Sin rarely starts with a massive explosion; it starts with a small spark. To fight sin, you must become a student of your own heart. What are your "triggers"?

✝ Is it **exhaustion** that leads to irritability?

✝ Is it **boredom** that leads to lust?

✝ Is it **insecurity** that leads to gossip?

When you identify the "gateway," you can set up defenses before the Enemy reaches the main fortress.

The Strategy of Displacement

You cannot leave a "void" in your soul. If you only focus on "not sinning," you will eventually fail. The secret to victory is what the old theologians called "the expulsive power of a new affection." You don't just stop loving sin; you start loving Jesus more.

✝ We fight **greed** with radical generosity.

✝ We fight **pride** with intentional service.

✝ We fight **anxiety** with the "living hope" of the Resurrection (Chapter 32).

The Use of the Word

Jesus showed us how to fight sin in the wilderness: He quoted Scripture. The Word of God is called the "Sword of the Spirit." It is the only offensive weapon we have. When a lie enters your mind (e.g., "God doesn't love you because you failed"), you don't fight it with a feeling; you fight it with a fact (e.g., "While we were still sinners, Christ died for us").

3. The Spiritual Gym: Growing Strong Through Disciplines

Strength in the Christian life is not a mystery; it is a result. Just as an athlete grows strong through repetitive training, the believer grows strong through **Spiritual Disciplines**. These are not "legalistic rules" to make God like us; they are "exercises" that make us more like God.

- ✝ **The Discipline of Intake:** Regularly saturating your mind with Scripture. If you are only "feeding" on the world's news and entertainment, you will be spiritually malnourished.

- ✝ **The Discipline of Silence:** Creating space to hear the "gentle whisper" of the Spirit (Chapter 41). In a world of constant noise, silence is a radical act of rebellion.

- ✝ **The Discipline of Fasting:** Voluntarily setting aside physical hunger to focus on spiritual hunger. It teaches the "Flesh" that it is not the boss.

- ✝ **The Discipline of Fellowship:** Realizing you cannot be "strong" alone. We are "built together" into a dwelling place for God.

4. The Armor of God: Clothed for the Day

In Ephesians 6, the Apostle Paul gives us a "check-list" for our daily spiritual attire. Notice that every piece of the armor is actually an application of the Gospel truths we have already studied.

1. **The Belt of Truth:** Knowing the objective "Map of Reality."

2. **The Breastplate of Righteousness:** Resting in your "Justification" (Chapter 38), not your own performance.

3. **The Shoes of Peace:** Walking in the "Reconciliation" (Chapter 31) provided by Christ.

4. **The Shield of Faith:** Trusting God's promises in the moment of "turbulence."

5. **The Helmet of Salvation:** Protecting your mind with the certainty of your future "Hope."

6. **The Sword of the Spirit:** The specific application of the Word to the situation at hand.

You don't "put on the armor" by saying a magic prayer; you put it on by **believing the Gospel** in the face of specific temptations. When you feel condemned, you put on the breastplate. When you feel hopeless, you put on the helmet.

5. Growing Strong in the "Middle"

One of the most dangerous myths in the Christian life is that "strong" means "never failing." In the Kingdom of God, strength is often found in the recognition of our weakness.

Paul asked God to remove his "thorn in the flesh," but God said, *"My grace is sufficient for you, for my power is made perfect in weakness"* (2 Corinthians 12:9). Growing strong means learning to lean more heavily on the Grace of God every day. It means that when you fall, you don't stay down; you repent, you look to the Cross, and you get back in the fight.

Strength is also a result of **Perseverance** (Chapter 40). We grow strong by enduring. Every time you choose to pray when you don't feel like it, every time you choose to be kind to an unkind person, and every time you choose to trust God in a trial, you are building "spiritual muscle." The "Map of Reality" assures us that this effort is never in vain.

6. Summary: The New Life Realized

As we conclude Part 7, look back at the journey. You have been called, born again, justified, and united to Christ. You have been given the Holy Spirit and a new identity. But all of this is for a purpose. You weren't saved just to go to heaven when you die; you were saved to be a "new kind of human" right now.

Walking in new life is the process of the "Inside" finally matching the "Outside." It is the slow, steady transformation of a rebel into a child, a slave into an heir, and a sinner into a saint. It is hard work, but it is the most rewarding work in the world. As you pray, fight sin, and grow strong, you are becoming a living witness to the power of the Gospel. You are showing the world what it looks like when God moves in.

Weekly Belief Statement

We believe that the Christian life is a spiritual warfare that requires constant vigilance, persistent prayer, and the active use of spiritual disciplines. We affirm that while we are secure in Christ, we must diligently put to death the deeds of the flesh and put on the full armor of God. We believe that spiritual strength is not self-generated but is the result of the Holy Spirit working through the means of grace as we faithfully follow our King.

Practical Application

✝ **The "Tactical Prayer":** Identify the one "battle" you are currently facing (e.g., a difficult relationship, a financial stress, a secret temptation). Spend 10 minutes today "radioing" the Commander. Don't just ask for the problem to go away; ask for the *strength* to represent Him well in the midst of it.

✝ **Audit Your "Gateway":** Spend 15 minutes in silence asking the Holy Spirit to show you the "spark" that leads to your most common sin. Once identified, create one "firewall" (e.g., "I will leave my phone in the other room at 10:00 PM").

✝ **Memorize the Armor:** This week, go through Ephesians 6:10–18 and connect each piece of armor to a chapter we have already read. Remind yourself that you are "clothed in Christ."

✝ **Read the Combat Manual:** Read the book of James. Notice how "down-to-earth" and "action-oriented" his instructions are. Pay attention to his warnings about the tongue and the heart.

✝ **Practice "The 10-Minute Discipline":** Pick one spiritual discipline you have been neglecting (e.g., silence or Bible intake) and commit to doing it for just 10 minutes every day this week. Don't look for immediate "feelings"; look for long-term "growth."

"Finally, be strong in the Lord and in the strength of his might." - Ephesians 6:10

PART EIGHT
Love the Church and Serve God's Mission

CHAPTER 43
Join the Church as God's Family

In our modern world, we tend to view spirituality as a deeply private, individual endeavor, something between "me and God." We live in an era of "on-demand" content, where we can listen to the best preachers in the world from our living rooms and sing along to worship playlists in our cars. Because of this, many people have come to believe a significant piece of misinformation: that the local church is an optional "extra" for the super-religious, rather than an essential part of the Christian life.

But if we look at the **Map of Reality**, we see a very different picture. When God rescues a person, He doesn't just save them *from* sin; He saves them *into* a community. You were not called to be a solitary soldier, but a member of an army. You were not adopted as an only child, but into a massive, global, and ancient family. In this chapter, we explore why joining the local church is not just a "good idea," but the natural and necessary environment for your spiritual survival and growth.

1. What is the Church? (Beyond the Brick and Mortar)

The first thing we must do is redefine our vocabulary. In common English, "church" usually refers to a building with a steeple. But in the New Testament, the Greek word is *ekklesia,* which means "a called-out assembly."

The Church is not a place you go; it is a people you belong to. It exists in two dimensions:

- **The Universal Church:** This is the "Total Map." It consists of every true believer in Jesus Christ across every nation, culture, and century. If you are in Christ, you are already a member of this spiritual body.

- **The Local Church:** This is the "Street-Level Map." It is a specific, local gathering of believers who meet regularly to worship, pray, and care for one another.

While the Universal Church is a glorious reality, you cannot "attend" the Universal Church. You cannot serve, be corrected by, or take the Lord's Supper with the Universal Church in the abstract. God's design is that every member of the Universal Church be functionally committed to a Local Church.

2. The Metaphor of Family: The Household of God

One of the most frequent ways the New Testament describes the Church is as a **family**. Paul tells Timothy that he is writing so that people will know how to behave in "the household of God" (1 Timothy 3:15).

This isn't just a sentimental metaphor; it is a legal and relational reality.

✝ **God is our Father:** Because of our adoption (Chapter 37), we have a common parentage.

✝ **Christ is our Elder Brother:** He is the firstborn among many brothers and sisters.

✝ **We are Siblings:** This means your relationship with other Christians is not based on shared hobbies, political views, or social status. It is based on shared blood, the blood of Christ.

In a family, you don't "consume" services; you share a life. Families have "messy" dinners, they have arguments, they support each other in sickness, and they carry each other's burdens. When you join a local church, you are saying, "These people are my brothers and sisters, and I am committed to them even when things get difficult."

3. The Metaphor of the Body: Radical Interdependence

Perhaps the most famous description of the Church is the **Body of Christ**. The Apostle Paul explains in 1 Corinthians 12 that just as a physical body has many parts (hands, feet, eyes, ears) that all need each other, so the Church is a single organism made up of many different people.

This metaphor teaches us three vital truths:

1. **Diversity:** We aren't all the same, and we shouldn't try to be. The body needs the "eye" to see and the "foot" to move.

2. **Necessity:** No part can say to the other, "I have no need of you." The most prominent preacher needs the quiet prayer warrior, and the talented musician needs the person who cleans the floors.

3. **Sympathy:** "If one member suffers, all suffer together; if one member is honored, all rejoice together" (1 Corinthians 12:26).

If you are not joined to a local body, you are like an amputated finger. You might still be "alive" in some sense, but you are not functioning, you aren't growing, and you are in a state of crisis. You need the body to survive, and the body, believe it or not, is missing something without you.

4. Correcting the "Lone Ranger" Myth

We must be direct: the idea of a "Churchless Christian" is foreign to the Bible. Throughout the New Testament, the "one anothers" (love one another, serve one another, rebuke one another, encourage one another) occur over 50 times. You cannot obey these commands in isolation.

Some say, "I can worship God alone in the woods." While you can certainly admire the Creator in nature, you cannot practice the humility of submission, the patience of forgiveness, or the sacrifice of service in the woods. The Church is the "gymnasium" where our spiritual muscles are worked out. Without the friction of other people, we don't grow; we just become self-centered.

5. The Messy Reality: A Hospital for Sinners

A common reason people avoid joining a church is "hypocrisy." They say, "The church is full of people who don't live what they preach."

Our response to this should be empathetic but firm: **You are absolutely right.** The Church is not a museum for saints; it is a hospital for sinners. It is a gathering of people who are "under construction" (Chapter 39). If you find a "perfect" church, don't join it, you'll ruin it!

The messiness of the church is actually part of its beauty. It is the place where God's grace is most visible because it's the place where we have to practice the hardest parts of the Gospel: forgiving those who hurt us and loving those who are difficult to love.

6. Why Formal Membership Matters

In a culture that is "commitment-phobic," the idea of formal church membership can feel restrictive. However, the Bible implies a level of commitment that goes beyond just showing up. The leaders of the church are told they will have to "give an account" for the souls in their care (Hebrews 13:17). This is only possible if they know *who* those souls are.

Membership is essentially a **Covenant.** It is a public way of saying:

✝ "I am responsible for you."

✝ "You are responsible for me."

✝ "We are following Jesus together."

It moves you from being a "spectator" to being a "participant." It moves the church from being a "vending machine" where you get your spiritual needs met, to being a family home where you share the chores and the joys.

7. The Benefits of Belonging

When you join the local church as God's family, you receive several "survival tools" for the Christian life:

✝ **Accountability:** We all have blind spots. We need brothers and sisters who love us enough to tell us when we are wandering off the map.

✝ **Protection:** Sheep are safest when they are in the fold under the care of shepherds (elders/pastors).

✝ **Encouragement:** The world is exhausting. The church is where we come to be reminded of the "Living Hope" (Chapter 32) by people who believe the same truths we do.

✝ **Discovery of Gifts:** You have been given spiritual gifts for the building up of others. You will likely never discover or use those gifts fully outside the context of the local church.

Weekly Belief Statement

We believe that the Church is the Body of Christ and the family of God, consisting of all true believers. We affirm that God's design for every Christian is to be a committed, active member of a local congregation. We believe that the local church is the primary place where we experience the "one anothers" of Scripture, exercise our spiritual gifts, and submit to the loving leadership and accountability that God has provided for our spiritual health and growth.

Practical Application

✝ **Evaluate Your Connection:** Are you a "consumer" or a "covenant member"? If you have been attending a church for a long time but haven't committed, pray about taking the step of formal membership this month.

✝ **The "Three-Person" Goal:** This week, don't just attend a service. Identify three people in your congregation and learn something meaningful about their lives. Move from "audience member" to "family member."

✝ **Read the "One Anothers":** Spend time this week reading Romans 12 and 1 Corinthians 12. Ask yourself: "How am I currently functioning as a part of the Body?"

✝ **Serve without a Title:** Look for a "low-glory" way to serve your local church family this week: straightening chairs, helping in the nursery, or staying late to clean up. Remember that in a family, everyone helps.

✝ **Pray for Your Leaders:** Your pastors and elders carry a heavy burden. Spend five minutes each day this week praying for their wisdom, their marriages, and their spiritual protection.

"So then you are no longer strangers and aliens, but you are fellow citizens with the saints and members of the household of God." - Ephesians 2:19

CHAPTER 44
Practice Church Life With Order and Love

If joining the church (Chapter 43) is like getting married, then *practicing* church life is the daily work of the marriage. It is one thing to have your name on a membership roll; it is quite another to navigate the rhythmic, sometimes friction-filled reality of living in a community of redeemed sinners. How do we prevent our "household of God" from becoming a house of chaos?

The answer provided by the New Testament is a beautiful, intentional blend of **Order** and **Love**. Without order, the church becomes a chaotic gathering where the loudest voices dominate and the mission is lost. Without love, the church becomes a cold, religious machine that grinds people down rather than lifting them up. In this chapter, we will explore the structural blueprint God has provided for His family, including the roles of leaders and the exercise of spiritual gifts, and why the "more excellent way" of love is the only thing that makes the structure work.

1. The Necessity of Divine Order

We live in an anti-institutional age. Many people prefer "organic" or "spontaneous" gatherings over structured ones. However, the Apostle Paul, writing to a very spontaneous and chaotic church in Corinth, gave this definitive rule:

> *"But all things should be done decently and in order"*
> *(1 Corinthians 14:40).*

God is not a God of confusion but of peace. In the original creation (Chapter 1), God brought order out of "tohu va-bohu" (formless and void). In the New Creation, the Church, He does the same. Order provides a "trellis" upon which the "vine" of the Gospel can grow. It ensures that the Word is preached accurately, the sacraments are administered faithfully, and the needs of the vulnerable are met consistently.

2. The Architecture of Leadership: Shepherds and Servants

To maintain this order, the New Testament establishes a clear, simple leadership structure. Church leadership is not about "power" or "prestige"; it is about **stewardship** and **service**. There are two primary "offices" described in Scripture:

Office	Primary Focus	Biblical Description
Elders (Pastors/ Overseers)	The Spiritual Health of the Body	Called to teach, pray, protect the flock from false doctrine, and provide spiritual oversight. They are the "Shepherds."
Deacons	The Physical Needs of the Body	Called to manage the practical affairs of the church, ensuring that the poor are cared for and the logistics of ministry are handled. They are the "Servants."

These leaders are not "above" the congregation in value; they are "among" the congregation in function. Their primary job is to "equip the saints for the work of ministry" (Ephesians 4:12). If your pastors are doing everything, the church is not functioning correctly. A healthy church is one where the leaders empower the members to use their own God-given gifts.

3. The Priesthood of All Believers: Your Role in the Order

One of the most radical truths of the Reformation was the rediscovery of the "Priesthood of All Believers." This means you do not need a "professional Christian" to mediate between you and God. It also means that *every* member of the church has a "ministry."

In the practice of church life, "order" means that everyone stays in their lane while moving toward the same goal. As we saw in the "Body" metaphor, the hand doesn't try to be an eye. When you find your place in the local church—whether that is teaching children, offering hospitality, or managing finances—you are contributing to the divine order. You aren't just a "member of the audience"; you are a "minister of the Gospel."

4. Corporate Worship: The Heartbeat of Church Life

The primary way we "practice" church life together is in the weekly gathering for worship. This is not a "concert" we attend, but a "liturgy" (the work of the people) we participate in. While different traditions have different styles, the "order" of a biblical service generally centers on four "elements":

1. **The Word Proclaimed:** The reading and preaching of Scripture is the "main course" of the meal. It is where we hear from our King.

2. **The Prayers Offered:** We lift our voices together in confession, petition, and praise.

3. **The Songs Sung:** We "address one another in psalms and hymns and spiritual songs" (Ephesians 5:19). Singing is a way we teach one another the Gospel.

4. **The Sacraments Shared:** Baptism and the Lord's Supper (which we will cover in the next chapters) are the "visible words" of the Gospel.

5. The "More Excellent Way": Love as the Essential Glue

You can have the most biblical leadership structure, the most eloquent preaching, and the most coordinated worship service, and still be a "noisy gong" or a "clanging cymbal." This is the warning of 1 Corinthians 13.

Love is not a "soft" emotion in the church; it is the "hard" commitment to prefer others over yourself. It is the "glue" that keeps the "order" from becoming legalistic. Paul's description of love is the ultimate "manual" for practicing church life:

✝ **Love is patient and kind:** It doesn't snap when the meeting goes long or a brother makes a mistake.

✝ **Love does not envy or boast:** It doesn't care who gets the credit for the new ministry project.

✝ **Love is not arrogant or rude:** It treats the newest member with the same respect as the senior pastor.

✝ **Love does not insist on its own way:** It is willing to yield on "non-essentials" for the sake of unity.

When we practice church life with love, we create an environment where it is safe to be "under construction." We create a culture where people can confess sin, admit doubt, and ask for help without fear of being discarded.

6. Navigating Conflict: The Test of Love

Because the church is a family of "recovered rebels," conflict is inevitable. Practicing church life with order and love means we don't "cancel" people when they offend us, nor do we sweep the offense under the rug.

We follow the "order" Christ gave in Matthew 18:

✝ We go to the person **privately** first.

✝ We go with the goal of **restoration**, not winning an argument.

✝ We assume the **best motives** in others until proven otherwise.

Conflict is often the "grist mill" God uses to produce the Fruit of the Spirit (Chapter 41) in us. You cannot learn patience without someone who tests your patience. You cannot learn forgiveness without an offense. In this way, the "messiness" of the church is not a distraction from our sanctification; it is the *means* of it.

7. The Power of Mutual Accountability

Finally, practicing church life means embracing the "one anothers." We are called to "exhort one another every day, as long as it is called 'today,' that none of you may be hardened by the deceitfulness of sin" (Hebrews 3:13).

In a healthy church order, we give others "permission" to speak into our lives. This is the ultimate act of love, to care enough about a brother or sister's soul to warn them when they are drifting. This "loving discipline" (which we will explore in Chapter 48) is not about punishment; it is about protection. It is the church acting as a "safety net" to catch us before we fall too far.

Weekly Belief Statement

We believe that the local church must be governed according to the order established in Scripture, primarily through the offices of Elders and Deacons. We affirm that corporate worship, the exercise of spiritual gifts, and mutual accountability are essential practices of the Christian life. We believe that love is the "more excellent way" that must animate all church activities, and we commit to pursuing the unity and peace of the body through humility, patience, and forgiveness.

Practical Application

✝ **Identify Your "Leaders":** Do you know who your elders and deacons are? Take a moment this week to write an encouraging note or email to one of them, thanking them for their "unseen" service.

✟ **Practice "Pre-Worship" Preparation:** Before you go to church this Sunday, spend 10 minutes in prayer. Ask God to give you a "hearing heart" for the Word and a "serving heart" for the people you will encounter.

✟ **The "One Another" Challenge:** Pick one of the "one another" commands (e.g., "Encourage one another" or "Bear one another's burdens") and focus on practicing it with one specific person in your church this week.

✟ **Audit Your "Love Level":** Read 1 Corinthians 13:4-7 slowly. Replace the word "Love" with your own name (e.g., "[Name] is patient, [Name] is kind..."). Where does the sentence feel like a lie? Ask the Holy Spirit to grow that specific trait in you.

✟ **Lean Into the "Order":** If your church has a "membership class" or a "small group" system, commit to participating. Don't just hover on the fringes; get into the "trellis" of the church structure so you can grow.

"Let all things be done for building up." -
1 Corinthians 14:26b

CHAPTER 45
Receive Baptism as a Sign of the Gospel

In the preceding chapters, we've explored the internal, invisible miracles of the Christian life: the "New Birth" (Chapter 37), "Justification" (Chapter 38), and "Union with Christ" (Chapter 37). These are tectonic shifts in the soul that the naked eye cannot see. However, God knows that we are not just "spirits"; we are physical creatures who live in a material world. We need tangible markers to anchor our faith.

This is where **Baptism** comes in. If the Gospel is a message to be heard, baptism is that same message "visible." It is the wedding ring of the Christian faith, an outward sign of an inward commitment and a physical seal of a spiritual reality. In this chapter, we explore why baptism is the "entry point" into the life of the church, what it actually symbolizes, and why receiving it is a joyful act of obedience for every follower of Jesus.

1. The Divine Mandate: Why We Baptize

Baptism is not a tradition invented by the church to make people feel included; it is a command issued by the King. In the "Great Commission," Jesus' final instructions to His disciples were:

"Go therefore and make disciples of all nations, baptizing them in the name of the Father and of the Son and of the Holy Spirit" (Matthew 28:19).

From the very first day of the Church at Pentecost, the pattern was clear: people heard the Gospel, they repented, and they were baptized. It is the "uniform" of the believer. To claim to follow Jesus while refusing baptism is a contradiction in terms, it would be like claiming to be a soldier while refusing to put on the fatigues. It is our public "Yes" to God's "Yes" to us.

2. The Meaning: A Triple Symbolism

Baptism is a rich, multi-layered "visible word." When someone is baptized, they are participating in a drama that tells three profound stories at once:

A. The Story of Cleansing

Water is the universal symbol of washing. Just as we use water to remove dirt from our bodies, baptism symbolizes the "washing away" of our sins. It points back to the promise in Ezekiel: *"I will sprinkle clean water on you, and you shall be clean from all your uncleannesses"* (Ezekiel 36:25). It is a visual reminder that because of Christ's blood, our record is clean.

B. The Story of Union (Death and Resurrection)

The Apostle Paul gives us the deepest theological meaning of baptism in Romans 6. He explains that when we are "baptized into Christ," we are spiritually participating in His death and resurrection.

✝ **Going under the water:** We are "buried" with Him. Our old, sinful self is dead and gone.

✝ **Coming out of the water:** We are "raised" with Him to walk in "newness of life."

Whether a church practices immersion (going all the way under) or pouring/sprinkling, the spiritual reality is the same: the old "you" is finished, and a new "you" has begun.

C. The Story of Incorporation

Baptism is the "door" into the local church family (Chapter 43). It is the moment you are formally "named." Notice that we are baptized into the **Name** (singular) of the **Father, Son, and Holy Spirit**. We are being adopted into the family of the Trinity and identified with the global and local people of God.

3. Sign vs. Reality: Does Water Save You?

This is a point where we must be direct and candid. A common piece of misinformation is that the act of baptism itself, the literal water on the skin, is what saves a person. This is often called "baptismal regeneration."

However, the "Map of Reality" teaches us that we are saved by **grace through faith** (Chapter 36), not by religious rituals.

✝ **The Sign:** The water and the act.

✝ **The Reality:** The Holy Spirit's work of regeneration in the heart.

Think of a wedding ring. Does the ring *make* you married? No. If you lose the ring, are you suddenly single? No. But if you are married, do you wear the ring? Absolutely. It is the sign that points to the covenant. Baptism doesn't "create" the relationship with God, but it "seals" and "signifies" it. We don't get baptized to *get* saved; we get baptized because we *are* saved.

4. The Subjects: Who Should Be Baptized?

Across the history of the church, there has been much debate about *who* should receive this sign.

✝ **Believer's Baptism (Credobaptism):** The view that baptism should only be given to those who have personally made a profession of faith. This emphasizes the "response" side of the Gospel.

✝ **Infant Baptism (Paedobaptism):** The view that baptism is the New Testament equivalent of circumcision, a sign of the covenant given to the children of believers, marking them as part of the "household of God" before they can even speak. This emphasizes the "promise" side of the Gospel.

Regardless of where your local church lands on this spectrum, the core truth remains the same: baptism is about **God's grace.** If you were baptized as an infant, your life's task is to "improve" that baptism by living out the faith it symbolized. If you were baptized as a believer, your task is to look back at that moment whenever you doubt God's love and remember: *"I have been named by Him."*

5. A Public Testimony in a Private World

In many parts of the world today, baptism is a dangerous act. In some cultures, you can tell people you "follow Jesus" and face little pushback, but the moment you are **baptized**, your family disowns you or the state persecutes you. Why? Because baptism is a public "defection" from the kingdom of this world to the Kingdom of God.

Even in a free society, baptism is a radical act of humility. You are standing before your community and saying: *"I am a sinner who needed washing. I am not my own; I belong to Jesus."* In an age of "personal branding" and "self-curation," baptism is the ultimate "un-branding." It is letting go of your image to take on His.

6. The Comfort of the Seal

One of the most beautiful aspects of baptism is that it is a **one-time event.** While we take the Lord's Supper repeatedly, we are only baptized once. This is because Christ died once and we are born again once.

When you go through seasons of "spiritual desert" or deep failure, your baptism stands as a permanent "seal" on your life. You can look back at that day and say, *"Even if I feel far from God right now, the water was real. The promise was real. I have been marked as His, and He does not lose what He has marked."* Martin Luther used to fight off depression and temptation by shouting to himself: *"I am baptized!"* He wasn't trusting in the water; he was trusting in the God who promised to be his Father in the water.

7. Why Wait?

If you have repented of your sins and placed your faith in Jesus, but you have not yet been baptized, the Bible's question to you is: *"Why do you wait? Rise and be baptized and wash away your sins, calling on his name"* (Acts 22:16).

Sometimes people wait because they don't feel "good enough" yet. But remember: baptism is a sign for *sinners*, not for the perfect. If you were perfect, you wouldn't need a "washing" sign! Others wait because they are shy or afraid of public speaking. But baptism is not a performance; it is a declaration of God's performance on your behalf. Don't let pride or fear keep you from the first step of obedience.

Weekly Belief Statement

We believe that baptism is an ordinance of the Lord Jesus, a sign of our fellowship with Him in His death and resurrection, of our being engrafted into Him, of remission of sins, and of our giving up ourselves to God through Jesus Christ to live and walk in newness of life. We affirm that while the water itself does not save, the act is a necessary and joyful response to the Gospel, serving as a visible seal of God's covenant promises to His people.

Practical Application

✠ The "Improvement" of Baptism: If you are already baptized, spend 10 minutes this week reflecting on that day. Ask yourself: *"How am I 'walking in newness of life' today as a result of the reality my baptism signaled?"*

✝ **The Bold Step:** If you have never been baptized, make an appointment this week to speak with a pastor or elder at your local church about taking this step. Don't wait for "perfect timing"; follow the King's command.

✝ **Witness the Drama:** The next time you see a baptism at your church, don't just "watch" it. "Renew" your own vows in your heart. Pray for the person being baptized, and thank God for the washing you have received in Christ.

✝ **Read the Narrative:** Read Acts 8:26–40 (the story of Philip and the Ethiopian eunuch). Notice the urgency and the joy associated with the eunuch's baptism.

✝ **The "Water Reminder":** Every time you wash your hands or take a shower this week, let the physical sensation of water remind you of the spiritual cleansing you have in Jesus. Say a short prayer: *"Thank You, Lord, for washing me clean."*

"Go therefore and make disciples of all nations, baptizing them in the name of the Father and of the Son and of the Holy Spirit." - Matthew 28:19

CHAPTER 46
Share the Lord's Supper With Faith

If baptism is the "front door" of the church, the **Lord's Supper** (also called Communion or the Eucharist) is the family dinner table. While we are baptized only once to mark our new birth, we return to the Lord's Table repeatedly throughout our lives. Why? Because while the Gospel is a message to be believed, God knows that we are prone to forget. We are "leaky vessels" who need to be constantly refilled with the truth of what Christ has done for us.

In this chapter, we transition from the "once-for-all" sign of entry to the "ongoing" sign of sustenance. The Lord's Supper is more than a religious snack or a somber halftime show in the middle of a worship service. It is a profound spiritual meal where we look backward in gratitude, upward in dependence, outward in unity, and forward in hope.

1. The Institution: A New Passover

The Lord's Supper did not appear out of thin air. It was born in the shadows of the **Passover**, the ancient Jewish meal that celebrated Israel's rescue from slavery in Egypt (Chapter 19). During His final meal with His disciples, Jesus took the traditional elements of the Passover, bread and wine, and radically redefined them.

He broke the bread and said, *"This is my body, which is given for you."* He took the cup and said, *"This cup that is poured out for you is the new covenant in my blood"* (Luke 22:19–20).

By doing this, Jesus was declaring that *He* was the true Passover Lamb. His death would not just rescue a single nation from a physical tyrant, but would rescue a global people from the spiritual tyranny of sin and death. He commanded us to "do this in remembrance of me," turning a historical meal into a perpetual memorial of the New Covenant.

2. The Three "Looks" of the Table

To share the Lord's Supper "with faith" is to engage our minds and hearts in three distinct directions at once.

A. Looking Backward: Remembrance

The Table is first and foremost a memorial. When we eat the bread and drink the cup, we are preaching the Gospel to ourselves. We are visually and physically reminding ourselves that our salvation was not free—it cost the broken body and spilled blood of the Son of God. We look back to the Cross and say, *"That was for me."*

B. Looking Upward: Spiritual Nourishment

This is where the "Real Presence" of Christ comes in. While denominations argue over *how* Jesus is present (physically or symbolically), the consensus of the historical Church is that he is **spiritually present** at the Table.

We do not just eat bread; by faith, we "feed on Christ." Just as physical bread gives strength to our bodies, the Spirit uses this meal to nourish our souls. It is a "means of grace" (Chapter 39) where God meets us, strengthens our faith, and confirms His promises to us.

C. Looking Forward: The Eternal Feast

Every time we take communion, we are practicing for a much larger party. Jesus said He would not drink the fruit of the vine again until He drinks it new in the Kingdom of God. The Lord's Supper is a "foretaste" of the **Marriage Supper of the Lamb** (Revelation 19). It reminds us that our story does not end in a graveyard, but at a feast. We eat the bread of "sorrow" now so that we can one day eat the bread of "joy" in the visible presence of our King.

3. The Table and the Body: Communion with One Another

The word "Communion" implies a shared reality. We do not take the Lord's Supper alone in a closet; we take it as an *ekklesia* (the assembly). In 1 Corinthians 10:17, Paul writes, *"Because there is one bread, we who are many are one body, for we all partake of the one bread."*

The Table is the great equalizer. At the Lord's Table, there are no social hierarchies, no racial divisions, and no political labels. The CEO and the janitor, the scholar and the child, all stand on the same ground: they are all beggars coming for the same bread.

If you are at odds with a brother or sister in the church, the Table becomes a place of conviction. You cannot truly be in communion with the Head (Christ) while you are actively rejecting a part of His Body (the Church). The Table demands that we pursue peace and unity within the local family.

4. Taking it "Worthily": The Call to Self-Examination

The Apostle Paul gives a stern warning in 1 Corinthians 11:27 about partaking in an "unworthy manner." This has caused many sensitive Christians to avoid the Table out of fear that they aren't "holy enough."

Let's be clear: **"Worthily" does not mean "perfectly."** If you had to be perfect to take communion, no one, including the pastor, could ever touch the bread. The only "worthy" way to come to the Table is to come as a self-confessed sinner who is desperate for grace.

To take the Supper in an *unworthy* manner means:

✟ **Ignoring the significance:** Treating it like common food or a thoughtless ritual.

✟ **Ignoring the Body:** Taking the bread while harboring bitterness or division against fellow believers.

✟ **Unrepentant sin:** Using the Table as a "cover" for a life of intentional rebellion against God.

Before we eat, we are called to "examine ourselves." We look inward, confess our recent failures, ask for forgiveness, and then, with joy, we eat the feast of the forgiven.

5. What Happens at the Table?

Perspective	What is happening?
The Legal	We are reminded that our debt is paid and our "Justification" (Chapter 38) is secure.
The Relational	We are enjoying a meal with our Father and our spiritual siblings.
The Transformative	We are receiving spiritual strength from the Holy Spirit to "Walk by the Spirit" (Chapter 41).
The Proclamatory	We are "proclaiming the Lord's death until he comes" to the watching world.

6. The Mystery and the Meal

There is a limit to how much we can explain about the Lord's Supper. It remains a "holy mystery." How can a small piece of bread and a sip of wine (or juice) carry so much weight? Because God has chosen to use the ordinary things of this world to convey the extraordinary things of His Kingdom.

In a digital age where everything is "virtual," the Lord's Supper is refreshingly physical. You can smell the bread; you can taste the fruit of the vine. It is God's way of saying, *"I didn't just save your soul; I saved you. And I will provide for you every step of the way."* > "This is a spiritual banquet, wherein Christ attests that He is the life-giving bread, by which our souls are fed unto true and blessed immortality." — *John Calvin*

7. The Practical Rhythm

The frequency of the Lord's Supper varies from church to church, some do it weekly, others monthly. The frequency is less important than the **disposition**. Every time the elements are passed, it is an opportunity to "reset" your spiritual compass.

If you have had a week of crushing failure, the Table says: *"Your failures are covered."* If you have had a week of spiritual pride, the Table says: *"You didn't earn this; it was a gift."* It keeps us centered on the only thing that actually matters: the person and work of Jesus Christ.

Weekly Belief Statement

We believe that the Lord's Supper is an ordinance of the New Testament, instituted by Jesus Christ, to be observed by His Church until the end of the world. We affirm that the bread and the cup are signs of His body and blood, and that as we partake of them by faith, we are spiritually nourished by Christ, we commemorate His death, we confirm our union with Him and with one another, and we anticipate His glorious return.

Practical Application

- **The "Pre-Table" Inventory:** On the morning before you take communion, spend 15 minutes in "self-examination." Ask: *"Is there any unconfessed sin I'm hiding? Is there any person in this church I am refusing to forgive?"* Bring those to the Lord before the service begins.

✝ **Focus on the "Now":** The next time you take the elements, try to avoid "autopilot." As you chew the bread, think: *"Jesus, Your body was broken for my wholeness."* As you drink the cup, think: *"Your blood was spilled for my cleansing."*

✝ **The "Horizontal" Glance:** Look around at the people taking communion with you. Specifically, look at someone you find difficult to get along with. Remind yourself: *"Christ died for them just as He died for me. We are one body."*

✝ **Read the Institution:** Read 1 Corinthians 11:17–34 this week. Notice how much Paul emphasizes the *unity* of the church in connection with the meal.

✝ **Meal-Time Gratitude:** At your next regular dinner at home, let the act of eating remind you of the Lord's Supper. Say a prayer of thanks not just for the physical food, but for the "Bread of Life" who sustains your soul.

"For as often as you eat this bread and drink the cup, you proclaim the Lord's death until he comes." -
1 Corinthians 11:26

CHAPTER 47
Serve God's Mission in the World

We have spent much of Part 8 focused inward, on the identity, order, and sacraments of the local church. It is easy, at this stage of the "Map of Reality," to view the church as a cozy fortress where we hide from the chaos of the world. But if the church is a "family home," it is one with no locks on the doors and a massive "Send" button in the foyer.

In this chapter, we pivot from the church's **gathering** to the church's **scattering**. We are moving from the dinner table to the harvest field. The Bible makes it clear that we are not just saved *from* our sins or *into* a family; we are saved **for** a mission. God is a missionary God, and His Church is His primary vehicle for reaching a broken, searching world. To live for God's glory means joining Him in His great rescue operation.

1. The Source: The Mission of God (*Missio Dei*)

Before the Church had a mission, God had a mission. From the moment the first human couple walked out of Eden (Chapter 16), God has been on a relentless pursuit to reconcile humanity to Himself.

✝ He called Abraham to be a blessing to "all the families of the earth" (Chapter 18).

✝ He sent prophets to call the nations to repentance.

✝ He sent His Son as the ultimate "Sent One" to bridge the gap.

The mission of the Church is simply a participation in the **Missio Dei** (The Mission of God). We don't have to "invent" a purpose for our lives or our churches; we simply have to look at what the Father is doing and join Him. As one theologian famously put it: *"It is not so much that God has a mission for His Church in the world, but that God has a Church for His mission in the world."*

2. The Mandate: The Great Commission

We have already seen the Great Commission in the context of baptism (Chapter 45), but now we look at it as the "Marching Orders" for every believer.

"All authority in heaven and on earth has been given to me. Go therefore and make disciples of all nations..."
(Matthew 28:18–19).

Notice the foundation: **Authority.** We don't go because we feel qualified; we go because Jesus is the King of the Universe. The mission is not an optional "elective" for the super-spiritual; it is the core curriculum of the Christian life.

What is a Disciple?

The goal of the mission is not just to "get people saved" (though that is the beginning). The goal is to "make disciples." A disciple is a **learner** and a **follower.** To make a disciple is to help someone move from being a stranger to God to being an apprentice of Jesus, learning to "observe all that He has commanded."

3. Salt and Light: The Twofold Strategy

Jesus used two common household items to describe our role in the world: **Salt** and **Light** (Matthew 5:13–16).

✝ **Salt (The Preservation):** In the ancient world, salt was used primarily to stop meat from rotting. As "salt," the Church acts as a preservative in society. We stand for truth, justice, and morality, slowing down the "rot" of sin in our cultures.

✝ **Light (The Illumination):** Light exposes what is hidden and shows the way. As "light," we don't just point out what is wrong; we show a better way to live. We illuminate the beauty of Christ through our deeds and our words.

Crucially, salt is useless if it stays in the saltshaker, and light is useless if it is hidden under a bowl. To be effective, the Christian must be **present** in the world: integrated into schools, workplaces, and neighborhoods, without becoming **polluted** by the world.

4. Word and Deed: The Two Wings of Mission

A common piece of misinformation in the modern church is that we must choose between **Evangelism** (sharing the Gospel) and **Social Action** (helping the poor and seeking justice). But in the "Map of Reality," these are the two wings of the same plane. If you remove one, the plane crashes.

Proclamation (Word)	Demonstration (Deed)
Telling people the "Good News" of Jesus.	Showing the "Good News" through mercy.
Addressing the spiritual need (Sin/Death).	Addressing the physical/social need (Poverty/Injustice).
Using our mouths to explain the Cross.	Using our hands to serve the broken.

If we only speak the Word but don't care for the poor, we are hypocrites. If we only do good deeds but never mention Jesus, we are just social workers with a fish on our cars. The mission of God is "holistic", it seeks the restoration of the whole person, body and soul.

5. Your Specific Calling: The Missionary in the Mirror

You might be thinking, *"I'm not a pastor, and I'm not moving to a jungle in another country. How can I serve the mission?"* This is where we must recover the **Cultural Mandate** (Genesis 1:28). God called humans to "fill the earth and subdue it." This means that your "secular" job is a platform for mission.

- ✝ If you are a **teacher**, you serve the mission by reflecting God's truth and loving your students.

- ✝ If you are a **plumber**, you serve the mission by bringing order out of chaos and working with integrity.

- ✝ If you are a **stay-at-home parent**, you are raising the next generation of the Kingdom.

The question isn't *"Am I a missionary?"* The question is *"Where is my mission field?"* Your neighborhood, your office, and your gym are the places where God has intentionally placed you to be salt and light.

6. To the Ends of the Earth: Global Concern

While we start "at home," we cannot stop there. The Great Commission is for **all nations** (Greek: *panta ta ethne*, all ethnic groups). There are still thousands of people groups in the world today who have no access to the Gospel, no Bible in their language, no church in their village.

A church that only cares about its own neighborhood is a church that has lost the heart of God. To serve the mission in the world means:

✝ **Praying** for the unreached.

✝ **Giving** sacrificially so that others can go.

✝ **Going** if God calls you to a different "map" entirely.

The "Map of Reality" is not complete until every tribe, tongue, and nation is represented around the throne of the Lamb.

7. The Power for the Mission

Finally, we must remember that we do not do this in our own strength. Jesus didn't just give the command; He gave the power. *"But you will receive power when the Holy Spirit has come upon you, and you will be my witnesses..."* (Acts 1:8).

The mission is not a "duty" we perform for a distant God; it is an adventure we participate in with a present Spirit. When you step out to share your faith or help someone in need, you are entering the "Spirit-empowered walk" (Chapter 41) at its highest level. You will find that God often shows up most clearly when you are at the end of your rope, trying to love someone who is hard to love or explain a truth you barely understand.

Weekly Belief Statement

We believe that the Church is sent into the world by Jesus Christ as He was sent by the Father. We affirm that the mission of the Church is to make disciples of all nations through the proclamation of the Gospel and the demonstration of God's love in works of mercy and justice. We believe that every Christian is called to be a witness for Christ in their specific sphere of influence, and that the Holy Spirit empowers us to fulfill this global task for the glory of God.

Practical Application

✝ **Identify Your "Mission Field":** Think of the three places where you spend the most time (e.g., your office, your coffee shop, your kid's soccer practice). Pray specifically for one person in each of those places this week.

✝ **The "Blessing" Challenge:** Seek to perform one "unseen" act of mercy this week for someone who can do nothing for you. Let it be a "demonstration" of the kindness of God.

✝ **Prepare Your "Word":** If someone asked you tomorrow, *"Why are you a Christian?"* or *"What is the Gospel?"*, could you explain it in two minutes? Practice your answer this week.

✝ **Read the Global Report:** Visit a website like the Joshua Project or Open Doors. Spend 15 minutes learning about an unreached people group or a persecuted church in another part of the world.

✝ **The "Monday Morning" Meditation:** Before you start work on Monday, pray: *"Lord, I am a missionary in this workplace today. Use my skill and my character to show Your glory."*

"But you will receive power when the Holy Spirit has come upon you, and you will be my witnesses in Jerusalem and in all Judea and Samaria, and to the end of the earth." - Acts 1:8

CHAPTER 48
Pursue Unity and Practice Loving Discipline

We have reached the final chapter of Part 8, and we are ending on what might be the most counter-cultural note in the entire "Map of Reality." In a world that prizes individual autonomy and "living your truth," the biblical concepts of **unity** and **discipline** can feel like relics of a bygone era.

However, if the Church is truly a family (Chapter 43) and a body (Chapter 44), then the health of the whole depends on the health of the parts. You cannot have a healthy family without boundaries, and you cannot have a functioning body if the cells are attacking each other. In this chapter, we explore how to fight for the unity Jesus prayed for and why the "hard grace" of church discipline is actually one of the most loving things a community can do for its members.

1. The High Stakes of Unity

On the night He was betrayed, Jesus didn't pray for the Church's success, wealth, or political influence. He prayed for our **unity**.

> *"...that they may all be one, just as you, Father, are in me,*
> *and I in you... so that the world may believe that you have*
> *sent me." (John 17:21)*

Unity is not just a "nice-to-have" feature; it is our primary apologetic. When a diverse group of people, divided by race, class, and politics, lives in radical harmony because of Jesus, the world is forced to take notice. Disunity, on the other hand, tells a lie about the Gospel. It suggests that the Cross isn't powerful enough to bridge human divides.

Unity vs. Uniformity

A common misconception is that unity means we all look, act, and think exactly alike. That isn't unity; that's **uniformity**.

✝ **Uniformity** is the result of external pressure (everyone wears the same "mask").

✝ **Unity** is the result of internal shared identity (different people, one Spirit).

2. The Trellis of Truth: Essentials and Non-Essentials

How do we maintain unity when we disagree? We must distinguish between different "levels" of truth. This is often described using the "theological triage" method:

Category	Level of Importance	Example
First-Order (Essentials)	The Gospel itself. To deny these is to deny the faith.	The Trinity, the Resurrection, Salvation by Grace.
Second-Order (Denominational)	Issues that affect how a church is organized.	Baptism (Chapter 45), Church Government (Chapter 44).
Third-Order (Opinions)	Issues where Christians can disagree and remain in the same local church.	End-times timelines, musical styles, political preferences.

Unity means standing firm on the essentials, being charitable on the second-order issues, and being flexible on the third-order opinions. As the famous maxim goes: *"In essentials, unity; in non-essentials, liberty; in all things, charity."*

3. The "Hard Grace" of Church Discipline

If unity is the goal, **loving discipline** is the guardrail that keeps us from falling off the cliff. Most people hear the word "discipline" and think of punishment or "shaming." But in the Bible, church discipline is a form of intensive care.

Why do we practice discipline?

1. **For the sake of the individual:** To wake them up to the danger of their sin and lead them to repentance.

2. **For the sake of the church:** To prevent sin from spreading like "leaven" through the community.

3. **For the sake of the world:** To protect the reputation of Jesus and the integrity of the Gospel.

Discipline is the "crook" on the Shepherd's staff. It's used to pull the sheep back when they are wandering toward a predator.

4. The Matthew 18 Process: The Way of Wisdom

Jesus gave us a specific, four-step "Map" for handling sin and conflict within the family (Matthew 18:15-17). The goal at every single step is **Restoration**, not excommunication.

1. **Private Confrontation:** If a brother sins against you, go to them *privately*. Most conflicts should die here. We don't post on social media; we talk face-to-face.

2. **Small Group Intervention:** If they won't listen, take one or two others along. This provides more perspectives and ensures the facts are clear.

3. **The Church Body:** If they still refuse to repent, it is brought before the leadership and the congregation. The weight of the family's concern is used to call them back.

4. **Exclusion (Excommunication):** This is the "last resort." If the person remains unrepentant in the face of the whole church, the church must acknowledge that the person is acting like an unbeliever and remove them from membership.

Even this final step is an act of love. It is the church saying: *"We love you too much to let you pretend you are following Jesus while you are living in open rebellion."*

5. The Spirit of the Fight

How we pursue unity and discipline matters as much as the actions themselves. Paul tells the Galatians:

> *"Brothers, if anyone is caught in any transgression, you who are spiritual should **restore him in a spirit of gentleness**" (Galatians 6:1).*

✝ **Self-Examination:** Before you confront a brother or sister, look at your own heart. Are you doing this because you're annoyed, or because you love their soul?

✝ **Patience:** Discipline shouldn't be rushed. It requires tears, prayer, and many conversations.

✝ **Forgiveness:** The moment a person repents, the discipline ends and the celebration begins. The Church must be as quick to forgive as it is slow to judge.

6. The Beauty of a "Pure" Church

When a church pursues unity and practices loving discipline, it becomes a safe place. It becomes a place where truth is actually spoken, where people are actually known, and where grace is actually experienced.

It is a "pure" church, not because the people are perfect, but because they are honest. They are a people who have decided that they love Jesus and each other too much to let sin go unaddressed. This kind of community is incredibly rare in 2026, and it is precisely what the "Map of Reality" calls us to build.

Weekly Belief Statement

We believe that the unity of the Spirit in the bond of peace is to be zealously maintained by all believers. We affirm that the local church has the responsibility to practice biblical discipline for the reclamation of wandering members, the purity of the body, and the honor of Christ's name. We commit to the Matthew 18 process, seeking always to restore the fallen in a spirit of gentleness and humility.

Practical Application

- **The "Gossip Kill":** This week, if someone tries to tell you about a "sin" or "conflict" involving a third party who isn't present, ask: *"Have you talked to them about this privately?"* If not, encourage them to follow Step 1 of Matthew 18.

- **The "Log" Check:** Before you get frustrated with the "disunity" in your church, read Matthew 7:1-5. Ask God: *"Is there a 'log' in my eye that is causing me to misjudge my brother?"*

- **Pray for the Wandering:** If you know someone who has walked away from the church or is living in unrepentant sin, spend 10 minutes praying for their "awakening." Ask the Holy Spirit to bring them to repentance.

- **Study the "One Anothers":** Review the list of "one another" commands. Which one are you currently finding the hardest to practice? (e.g., "Bearing with one another" or "Forgiving one another").

- **Thank Your Leaders:** Church discipline is the hardest part of a pastor's job. If you know your leaders are currently navigating a difficult situation, send them a note letting them know you are praying for their wisdom and courage.

PART NINE
Live With Hope

CHAPTER 49
Face Death With Christian Hope

In the modern world, death is often treated as the ultimate "glitch" in the system, a dark, silent wall that we spend our lives trying to ignore, delay, or medicate. We hide it behind the sterile walls of hospitals and the euphemisms of funeral parlors. But for the person living by the **Map of Reality**, death is not a wall; it is a doorway.

As we enter Part 9, we turn our gaze toward the horizon. If the previous sections showed us how to live, this section shows us how to hope. To "Face Death With Christian Hope" is not to pretend that death isn't sad or painful, even Jesus wept at the tomb of His friend. Rather, it is to realize that for the believer, death has been "swallowed up in victory." In this chapter, we explore the sting of death, the intermediate state of the soul, and why the Christian can walk into the valley of the shadow without fear.

1. The Anatomy of the Enemy: Why Death Exists

To have a true hope, we must first have a true diagnosis. Death was not part of God's "very good" original design (Chapter 1). It is an intruder.

As we saw in Chapter 16, death is the "wage" of sin. It is the tragic tearing apart of what God joined together: the human soul and the human body. Because we are embodied souls, the separation of the two feels like a violent rip in the fabric of our being. This is why we feel a natural, healthy revulsion toward death. It is an "enemy", the "last enemy," according to the Apostle Paul.

2. The Defeated Foe: How Christ Changed the Map

The reason Christians can face death differently is that our King has already gone through it and come out the other side.

By His death, Jesus paid the "wage" we owed. By His resurrection, He broke the power of the grave. The "Map of Reality" has been fundamentally redrawn: Death is no longer a prison warden, but a transition officer.

For the believer, the "sting" of death, which is sin and the judgment of the law, has been removed. Death can still hurt us, and it can still take us, but it can no longer **defeat** us. It is like a bee that has lost its stinger; it may buzz loudly and cause us to flinch, but it cannot deliver a fatal blow.

3. The Intermediate State: "Absent from the Body, Present with the Lord"

A common question arises: *What happens to us the second we die?* While we wait for the final Resurrection, what is the state of the believer between death and the end of the world?

The Bible calls this the "Intermediate State." It teaches that while our bodies go into the ground to wait for the resurrection, our souls go immediately into the presence of Jesus.

✝ Paul says his desire was to "depart and be with Christ, for that is far better" (Philippians 1:23).

✝ Jesus told the thief on the cross, "Today you will be with me in paradise" (Luke 23:43).

✝ 2 Corinthians 5:8 tells us that to be "away from the body" is to be "at home with the Lord."

This is not a "sleep" where we are unconscious; it is a conscious, joyful rest. We are "at home." We are finally free from the presence of sin, the struggle of the flesh, and the pains of this life.

4. Grieving with Hope

One of the most significant pieces of misinformation about Christian hope is that "real Christians don't cry at funerals." This is false and harmful.

The Apostle Paul tells us not to grieve **as others do who have no hope** (1 Thessalonians 4:13). He does *not* say "don't grieve." We grieve the separation. We grieve the loss of a voice, a touch, and a shared history. But our grief is "shot through" with hope.

✝ We grieve as those who know the separation is temporary.

✝ We grieve as those who know the story isn't over.

✝ We grieve as those who know their loved one is currently more "alive" than they have ever been.

5. Preparing for the Final Enemy

Facing death with hope is not just about how we feel at a funeral; it is about how we live today. Knowing that our "title deed" to eternal life is secure (Chapter 38) changes our relationship with our time, our money, and our fears.

✝ **It frees us from the "Bucket List" mentality:** We don't have to cram every possible experience into this life because this life is just the "preface" to the real story.

✝ **It gives us courage:** If the worst thing that can happen to us (death) results in the best thing that can happen to us (seeing Jesus), then what do we really have to fear from the world?

✝ **It shifts our perspective on suffering:** We realize that our "light momentary affliction is preparing for us an eternal weight of glory" (2 Corinthians 4:17).

6. The "Art of Dying Well"

Throughout church history, Christians practiced the *Ars Moriendi*, the art of dying. This meant living in such a way that when death came, they were ready. To die well in the "Map of Reality" means:

1. **Ensuring your trust is in Christ alone:** Not in your "good life" or your religious attendance.

2. **Tying up loose ends:** Forgiving those who have hurt you and seeking reconciliation where possible.

3. **Passing on the Map:** Using your final days or years to tell the next generation about the faithfulness of God.

Death is the final opportunity on earth to testify that Jesus is enough. When a Christian faces death with a quiet, steady peace, it is one of the most powerful witnesses to the truth of the Gospel.

Weekly Belief Statement

We believe that death is the result of sin and the last enemy to be destroyed. We affirm that for those who are in Christ, the sting of death has been removed by His victory. We believe that at death, the souls of believers pass immediately into the presence of Christ in a state of conscious joy and rest, while their bodies wait in the grave for the final resurrection. We commit to grieving with hope and living with the courage that comes from knowing our true life is hidden with Christ in God.

Practical Application

✟ **The "Legacy" Meditation:** Imagine you were told you had one month to live. What are the three most important things you would want to say to the people you love? Write those things down today. Why wait?

✟ **Comfort the Grieving:** Reach out to someone you know who has lost a loved one recently. Don't try to "fix" their pain with clichés. Simply sit with them, acknowledge the "enemy" of death, and remind them (gently) of the "doorway" of hope.

✟ **Read the "Final Words":** Read the account of the death of Stephen in Acts 7:54-60. Notice where his eyes were fixed as he faced death.

✟ **The "Cemetery Walk":** Sometime this week, walk through a local cemetery. Don't view it as a place of gloom, but as a "dormitory"—a place where bodies are "sleeping" until the King calls them awake.

✟ **Memorize the Victory Shout:** Memorize 1 Corinthians 15:55-57: *"O death, where is your victory? O death, where is your sting? ... But thanks be to God, who gives us the victory through our Lord Jesus Christ."*

"Precious in the sight of the Lord is the death of his saints."
- Psalm 116:15

CHAPTER 50
Expect the Resurrection and the New Earth

If you were to ask the average person on the street what happens at the "end" of the Christian story, they would likely describe a scene of disembodied souls floating on clouds in a misty, ethereal "heaven." This vision of the afterlife is common, but it is a significant piece of misinformation. The Bible's "Map of Reality" does not end with us leaving the earth to live as ghosts; it ends with God coming down to earth to live with us as resurrected, physical people.

In this chapter, we move from the "Intermediate State" to the final, glorious climax of the human story. We will explore the promise of the **Resurrection of the Body** and the restoration of all things in the **New Earth**. This is the hope that anchors the soul: that everything broken will be mended, and everything lost will be found.

1. The Resurrection of the Body: Life 2.0

The Apostles' Creed concludes with the phrase, "I believe in the resurrection of the body." This is the foundational hope of the New Testament. We do not just believe in the "immortality of the soul"; we believe that the same God who knit your body together in your mother's womb (Chapter 14) intends to put it back together, better than ever.

Like the Firstfruits

Our blueprint for this hope is the Resurrection of Jesus. He was not a ghost; He ate fish, He could be touched, and He had a recognizable voice. Yet, He was also different, He was no longer subject to pain, aging, or death. Paul calls Jesus the "firstfruits" (1 Corinthians 15:20). Just as the first ripe apple on a tree proves that a whole harvest is coming, Jesus' resurrection proves that ours is coming too.

Continuity and Transformation

When the King returns, the "dead in Christ" will rise first. Your resurrected body will be **you**, but the "best version" of you.

✝ **Continuity:** It is your body, your history, and your identity.

✝ **Transformation:** It is a body "raised in power." No more glasses, no more cancer, no more depression, no more decay. It is a body perfectly suited for an eternal, physical existence.

2. The New Earth: Heaven Comes Down

Many Christians live as if the physical world is a "disposable wrapper" for the soul. But God is a Creator who loves His craftsmanship. He does not plan to scrap the earth and start over; He plans to **redeem** and **renew** it.

In Revelation 21, John sees a vision not of us going up, but of the "New Jerusalem" coming *down* out of heaven to earth. The end of the Bible looks a lot like the beginning, a Garden-City where God walks with His people.

> "And I heard a loud voice from the throne saying, 'Behold, the dwelling place of God is with man. He will dwell with them, and they will be his people...'" (Revelation 21:3)

A Physical Reality

The New Earth will be a place of colors, sounds, tastes, and meaningful work. We will have feasts, we will build, we will create, and we will explore. All the beauty of this current world, the mountains, the music, the laughter, is just a "trailer" for the feature film that is the New Earth.

3. The Reversal of the Curse

In the New Earth, the "Map of Reality" is finally cleared of every "glitch" introduced in Genesis 3. The "four-fold brokenness" (Chapter 16) is completely healed.

✝ **No more pain:** The nervous system will no longer carry signals of agony.

✝ **No more sorrow:** "He will wipe away every tear from their eyes." This implies that God personally comforts us for the pains of the "Old Earth."

✝ **No more death:** The grave is permanently closed.

✝ **No more sin:** Our "Walk by the Spirit" (Chapter 41) will be effortless because our hearts will be perfectly aligned with God's.

4. The Cosmic Scope of Redemption

We often think salvation is only about human souls. But Romans 8:21 tells us that "the creation itself will be set free from its bondage to corruption."

Animals, plants, and the very stars themselves are waiting for the "revealing of the sons of God." When the King returns and His people are resurrected, the entire physical universe will receive an "upgrade." The decay of entropy will be replaced by the vitality of eternal life. The New Earth is not a "consolation prize"; it is the "Grand Prize" of God's redemptive plan.

5. Why This Matters Today: The Power of Anticipation

Expecting the resurrection and the New Earth is not "escapism." In fact, it is the only thing that makes it possible to engage deeply with this world without losing heart.

1. **It Validates the Physical:** If God is going to resurrect our bodies and renew the earth, then what we do with our bodies and how we treat the earth *matters.*

2. **It Sustains Us in Suffering:** A person with a "Resurrection Hope" can endure a disability, a chronic illness, or the loss of a limb knowing that it is a temporary condition. The "Map" says: *Your healing is coming.*

3. **It Reorders Our Ambitions:** We don't have to "have it all" now. We can be generous and sacrificial today because we know we have an eternity of abundance ahead of us.

6. The Beatific Vision: Seeing His Face

The greatest joy of the New Earth is not the lack of pain or the beauty of the scenery. It is the **Beatific Vision.**

"They will see his face" (Revelation 22:4).

Throughout the "Old Earth," we see God through a glass darkly, through the Word, through the Spirit, and through the Church. But in the New Earth, the "cloud" is removed. We will see the King in His beauty. This is the "End" for which we were made: to look upon the infinite beauty of God and be satisfied forever.

Weekly Belief Statement

We believe in the bodily resurrection of the dead at the return of Jesus Christ. We affirm that God will create a New Heaven and a New Earth in which righteousness dwells, and where He will live with His people forever. We believe that this future hope is a physical, tangible reality where sin, death, and decay are no more, and where the glory of God will be our light and our joy.

Practical Application

- ✟ **The "Sensory Prayer":** Go outside and find something beautiful in nature (a flower, a sunset, a tree). Thank God for it, and then say: *"Lord, I can't wait to see the 'New Earth' version of this."*

- ✟ **Comfort the Broken-Bodied:** If you or someone you know is struggling with a physical limitation or illness, meditate on 1 Corinthians 15:42-44. Remind yourself that the "seed" being sown in weakness will be raised in power.

- ✟ **Audit Your "Heaven" Vision:** Have you been thinking of the afterlife as a "misty cloud"? This week, try to visualize the New Earth as a place of vibrant colors, solid ground, and shared meals. Read Revelation 21-22 aloud to help your imagination.

- ✟ **The "Investment" Shift:** Look at one physical possession you value. Remind yourself: *"This will pass away, but the person I am becoming in Christ will live forever."* Use this to loosen your grip on material things.

- ✟ **Practice Resurrection Joy:** Choose one "hopeless" situation in your life or neighborhood. Pray for it with the confidence that God is in the business of bringing life out of death.

"He will wipe away every tear from their eyes, and death shall be no more, neither shall there be mourning, nor crying, nor pain anymore, for the former things have passed away." - Revelation 21:4

CHAPTER 51
Prepare for Final Judgment and Eternal Life

As we approach the end of the **Map of Reality**, we must face a truth that is both sobering and deeply comforting: there is a day of reckoning coming. In our modern culture, the idea of "judgment" is often viewed with hostility or dismissed as an archaic threat. However, without a final judgment, there is no ultimate justice. If the curtain simply falls on history without every wrong being addressed and every truth being revealed, then the "Map" is fundamentally broken.

In this chapter, we look at the reality of the **Final Judgment** and the two eternal destinies that follow: **Eternal Life** in the presence of God and **Eternal Separation** from Him. This is the moment where every human story is finalized. For the believer, this is not a day to be feared, but a day to be prepared for with "sober joy."

1. The Necessity of Judgment

Why must there be a judgment? Because God is perfectly Holy and perfectly Just. Throughout history, millions of people have suffered under tyrants who were never caught, and millions of "small" sins have gone unnoticed by human eyes.

If God did not judge, He would not be good. A judge who looks at a crime and says "it doesn't matter" is a corrupt judge. The Final Judgment is the moment where the King of the Universe steps onto the stage to "set the world right." It is the ultimate "audit" of human history.

> *"For we must all appear before the judgment seat of*
> *Christ, so that each one may receive what is due for what*
> *he has done in the body, whether good or evil."*
> *(2 Corinthians 5:10)*

2. The Great White Throne: The Standard of Truth

The Bible describes a scene where "the books are opened" (Revelation 20:12). This represents God's perfect knowledge. Nothing is hidden from His sight, not our public actions, our private words, or the secret intentions of our hearts.

The Two Books

Scripture speaks of two different sets of records:

- **The Books of Deeds:** These contain the record of every life. For those standing on their own merit, this is the standard. Since God's standard is perfect holiness, no one can survive this "audit" based on their own performance (Chapter 36).

- **The Lamb's Book of Life:** This contains the names of those who are united to Jesus Christ by faith.

3. How the Believer Faces Judgment

If we have all sinned, how can a Christian face this day with anything but terror? The answer lies in **Justification** (Chapter 38).

When a believer stands before the judgment seat, they do not stand alone. Their "defense attorney" is also their Judge. Because Christ took our judgment upon Himself on the Cross, the "verdict" for the believer has already been handed down: **Not Guilty.** For the Christian, the Final Judgment is not about *salvation* (that was settled at the Cross); it is about **vindicaton** and **rewards.**

- **Vindication:** It is the day the world finally sees that your faith was not in vain and that you belong to the King.

- **Evaluation:** Our lives as believers will be evaluated for how we used the gifts, time, and resources God gave us. This results in "rewards" or "crowns," which are ultimately just more capacity to glorify God.

4. The Reality of Eternal Separation (Hell)

We must address the most difficult part of the Map: the reality of **Hell.** Many find this doctrine offensive, but it is the logical result of human free will and God's justice.

Hell is not a place where God "sends" people who desperately want to be with Him; it is the place where God finally grants people the "autonomy" they have asked for all their lives. If someone spends their life saying to God, "Leave me alone," God eventually says, "Thy will be done."

✞ **The Nature of Hell:** It is described as "outer darkness" and "eternal destruction." It is the total absence of the common grace, beauty, and love of God.

✞ **The Misinformation:** Hell is not a place where the Devil is in charge wearing a red suit; it is a place of judgment for the Devil and his angels, and all who follow his rebellion.

As C.S. Lewis famously said: *"There are only two kinds of people in the end: those who say to God, 'Thy will be done,' and those to whom God says, in the end, 'Thy will be done.'"*

5. The Reality of Eternal Life (Heaven)

On the other side of the judgment is **Eternal Life**. As we saw in Chapter 50, this is not a boring, static existence. It is the beginning of the "Real Story."

✞ **Infinite Discovery:** Because God is infinite, our "knowing" of Him will never end. We will go deeper and deeper into His beauty and wisdom forever.

✞ **Perfect Communion:** We will live in a society where there is no pride, no jealousy, and no misunderstanding.

✞ **Total Satisfaction:** The "thirst" of the human soul that we have tried to quench with money, sex, or power will finally be satisfied at the "Fountain of Living Water."

6. Preparation: Living for the "Well Done"

How then should we live today in light of the coming judgment? We should live with **Eternal Perspective**.

If you knew that in one year all your current currency would become worthless and be replaced by a new one, you would spend the year converting your wealth. The Final Judgment is the "currency exchange" of the universe.

✞ **Invest in people:** They are the only things that last forever.

✞ **Invest in character:** It is the only thing you "take with you."

✞ **Live in the Light:** Knowing that everything will be revealed, we practice radical honesty and repentance now.

The goal of the Christian life is to hear those five words from the King: *"Well done, good and faithful servant."*

Weekly Belief Statement

We believe that God has appointed a day in which He will judge the world in righteousness by Jesus Christ. We affirm that all people will be resurrected, some to eternal life in the presence of God, and others to eternal punishment and separation from Him. We believe that for those in Christ, the judgment is a day of vindication and reward, as we are covered by the righteousness of our Savior. We commit to living each day in the light of eternity, seeking to please our King in all we do.

Practical Application

- **The "Motives" Audit:** Pick one "good thing" you do this week (like serving at church or giving to charity). Ask yourself: *"If this were revealed at the Final Judgment, what would the books say about my motive?"* Bring that motive to God in prayer.

- **Practice Immediate Repentance:** Since everything will be brought to light eventually, "clear the deck" today. If you have a secret sin, confess it to God and a trusted brother or sister now.

- **The "Reward" Shift:** When you are overlooked or unappreciated for a good deed this week, remind yourself: *"The Judge sees, and His 'Well Done' is the only one that matters."*

- **Read the Vision:** Read Matthew 25:31-46. Notice that the King identifies Himself with "the least of these." How does the reality of judgment change how you treat the poor or the lonely?

- **A Prayer for the Lost:** Spend 5 minutes praying for someone you know who does not yet have their name in the Book of Life. Ask God for an opportunity to share the "Map" with them before the day of judgment arrives.

"Now there is in store for me the crown of righteousness, which the Lord, the righteous Judge, will award to me on that day—and not only to me, but also to all who have longed for his appearing." - 2 Timothy 4:8

CHAPTER 52
Live for the New Creation Today

We have reached the end of our journey through the **Map of Reality**. We have traveled from the "Deep Past" of creation and the fall, through the "Great Rescue" of the Cross, into the "Daily Walk" of the Spirit, and finally to the "High Peaks" of the Resurrection and the New Earth. But as we close this map, a final question remains: *Now what?*

If the New Creation is a future reality, does that mean we just sit in a "spiritual waiting room" until the King returns? Far from it. In this final chapter, we discover that the New Creation has already broken into the present. To live as a Christian is to be a "colony of heaven" in a foreign land, bringing the values, the joy, and the life of the future world into the "here and now."

1. The "Already" and the "Not Yet"

To understand how to live today, we must master the tension of the **Already/Not Yet.**

> **Already:** Jesus has risen. The Holy Spirit has been poured out. You are already a "new creation" in Christ (2 Corinthians 5:17).

> **Not Yet:** Our bodies still age. Sin still persists in the world. The King has not yet physically returned to set all things right.

Living for the New Creation means living in that "overlap." We don't wait for the New Earth to start acting like citizens of the New Earth. We begin the "resurrection life" today.

2. Signposts of the Future

Imagine you are driving to a beautiful city. Long before you arrive, you see signs that say "100 miles," "50 miles," and then "Welcome to..."

The Church is called to be a **signpost** for the New Creation. When people look at our lives and our communities, they should get a "preview" of what the coming Kingdom looks like.

✝ Where the world is **divided**, we show the **unity** of the New Creation.

✝ Where the world is **hopeless**, we show the **joy** of the Resurrection.

✝ Where the world is **exploitative**, we show the **justice** and **generosity** of the King.

3. Redeeming the Ordinary

One of the most powerful ways we live for the New Creation is by refusing to see anything as "meaningless." Because Christ is reclaiming the physical world (Chapter 50), everything we do in the body matters.

✝ **Work:** We work with excellence because we are practicing for the meaningful activity of the New Earth.

✝ **Art and Beauty:** We create music, stories, and art that reflect the beauty of God, whispering to the world that there is more to the story than decay.

✝ **Rest:** We practice the Sabbath as a weekly "mini-foretaste" of the eternal rest we will enjoy with God.

When you fix a broken car, plant a garden, or care for a child, you are doing "New Creation work." You are pushing back the "tohu va-bohu" (chaos) and bringing a small piece of God's order into the world.

4. Loving the "Un-Renewed"

Living for the New Creation changes how we look at people. We no longer see people as they are in their brokenness, but as who they could be in Christ.

C.S. Lewis famously said, *"There are no ordinary people. You have never talked to a mere mortal."* Every person you meet is an eternal being who will one day either be a "bright, resurrected splendor" or a "shattered, tragic ruin." Living for the New Creation means treating every human being with the dignity and weight they deserve as image-bearers of God. It means loving the "un-renewed"—the difficult, the broken, and the enemy— because that is exactly how God loved us.

5. The Posture of Prayer: "Thy Kingdom Come"

Our primary heartbeat as we live for the New Creation is the prayer Jesus taught us: *"Thy Kingdom come, Thy will be done, on earth as it is in heaven."* This is a revolutionary prayer. It is an invitation for the "Map of Heaven" to be overlaid onto the "Map of Earth."

✝ When we see **injustice**, we pray: *"Kingdom come here."*

✝ When we see **sickness**, we pray: *"Kingdom come here."*

✝ When we see **our own sin**, we pray: *"Kingdom come here."*

We live with a "divine discontent." We are grateful for God's grace today, but we are hungry for the full restoration that is coming.

6. The Final Word: Maranatha

The very last prayer in the Bible is a short, Aramaic word: **Maranatha.** It means, *"Come, Lord Jesus!"* (Revelation 22:20).

As you fold up this "Map of Reality," let that be your final posture. We are a people of the **Return**. We live with our bags packed and our lamps lit. We aren't afraid of the future because we know who holds the future. We know that the King who died for us is the King who is coming for us.

The story of the Map of Reality ends not with an "Exit" sign, but with an "Entrance." The best is yet to come.

Weekly Belief Statement

We believe that the New Creation has already begun in the resurrection of Jesus Christ and the gift of the Holy Spirit. We affirm that as believers, we are called to live as citizens of the coming Kingdom in the present age, seeking God's will on earth as it is in heaven. We commit to working, loving, and serving in a way that provides a visible signpost to the world of the glorious restoration that God will complete at the return of our King.

Practical Application

✝ **The "Restoration" Project:** Find one small thing in your immediate world that is "broken" (a relationship, a messy room, a neighbor's need). Commit to bringing "New Creation order" to that thing this week as an act of worship.

✝ **The "Resurrection" Greeting:** Practice looking at the people you encounter this week through the lens of eternity. Remind yourself: *"This person is an eternal being."* See how it changes your patience and kindness toward them.

✝ **Set Your "Compass":** Each morning this week, pray the first half of the Lord's Prayer: *"Our Father... Your Kingdom come."* Specifically ask God to bring His Kingdom into one area of your life that feels chaotic.

✝ **Read the Ending:** Read Revelation 21 and 22 slowly. Let the physical descriptions of the New Earth sink into your imagination and fuel your hope for the week.

✝ **The "Maranatha" Breath:** Throughout the day, when you feel stressed or overwhelmed by the "Old World," take a deep breath and whisper: *"Maranatha. Come, Lord Jesus."* Let it ground you in the truth that the struggle is temporary and the King is near.

CONCLUSION
Keep Growing After Week 52: Build a Life Shaped by Truth

You have reached the end of this "Map of Reality," but in the Kingdom of God, an end is always a beginning. These fifty-two chapters were never meant to be a mere intellectual exercise or a box to check. They were designed to provide the "trellis" upon which the vine of your spiritual life can grow.

The Christian life is not a sprint; it is a long-distance journey of **becoming**. Now that you have the map, the goal is to live within its borders.

- **Stay in the Word:** The Map is only useful if you continue to consult the Original Text, the Holy Scriptures.

- **Stay in the Family:** As we saw in Chapter 43, you cannot walk this terrain alone. Lean into your local church.

- **Stay in the Spirit:** Keep the rhythm of "keeping in step" (Chapter 41) as your daily heartbeat.

The world will constantly try to hand you a different, smaller map, one based on self-interest, fear, or temporary pleasure. Resist it. Keep your eyes on the King, your heart in the Truth, and your feet moving toward the New Creation.

APPENDICES

Appendix A: The Apostles' Creed

The oldest and most widely used summary of the Christian faith, focusing on the basics of the Gospel.

I believe in God, the Father almighty, creator of heaven and earth. I believe in Jesus Christ, his only Son, our Lord, who was conceived by the Holy Spirit and born of the virgin Mary. He suffered under Pontius Pilate, was crucified, died, and was buried; he descended to hell. The third day he rose again from the dead. He ascended to heaven and is seated at the right hand of God the Father almighty. From there he will come to judge the living and the dead. I believe in the Holy Spirit, the holy catholic* church, the communion of saints, the forgiveness of sins, the resurrection of the body, and the life everlasting. Amen.

**The word "catholic" here refers to the universal church, not a specific denomination.*

Appendix B: The Nicene Creed

Drafted in AD 325 and 381, this creed provides a deeper theological definition of the Trinity and the nature of Christ.

We believe in one God, the Father, the Almighty, maker of heaven and earth, of all that is, seen and unseen.

We believe in one Lord, Jesus Christ, the only Son of God, eternally begotten of the Father, God from God, Light from Light, true God from true God, begotten, not made, of one Being with the Father; through him all things were made. For us and for our salvation he came down from heaven, was incarnate from the Holy Spirit and the Virgin Mary and was made man. For our sake he was crucified under Pontius Pilate; he suffered death and was buried. On the third day he rose again in accordance with the Scriptures; he ascended into heaven and is seated at the right hand of the Father. He will come again in glory to judge the living and the dead, and his kingdom will have no end.

We believe in the Holy Spirit, the Lord, the giver of life, who proceeds from the Father and the Son, who with the Father and the Son is worshiped and glorified, who has spoken through the prophets. We believe in one holy catholic and apostolic Church. We acknowledge one baptism for the forgiveness of sins. We look for the resurrection of the dead, and the life of the world to come. Amen.

Appendix C: The Definition of Chalcedon

Adopted in AD 451, this document clarifies the "Hypostatic Union"—how Jesus is both fully God and fully man.

Therefore, following the holy fathers, we all with one accord teach men to acknowledge one and the same Son, our Lord Jesus Christ, at once complete in Godhead and complete in manhood, truly God and truly man, consisting also of a reasonable soul and body; of one substance with the Father as regards his Godhead, and at the same time of one substance with us as regards his manhood; like us in all respects, apart from sin; as regards his Godhead, begotten of the Father before the ages, but as regards his manhood begotten, for us men and for our salvation, of Mary the Virgin, the God-bearer; one and the same Christ, Son, Lord, Only-begotten, recognized in **two natures, without confusion, without change, without division, without separation**; the distinction of natures being in no way annulled by the union, but rather the characteristics of each nature being preserved and coming together to form one person and subsistence, not as parted or separated into two persons, but one and the same Son and Only-begotten God the Word, Lord Jesus Christ.

Check out another book in the series

Welcome Aboard, Check Out This Limited-Time Free Bonus!

Ahoy, reader! Welcome to the Ahoy Publications family, and thanks for snagging a copy of this book! Since you've chosen to join us on this journey, we'd like to offer you something special.

Check out the link below for a FREE e-book filled with delightful facts about American History.

But that's not all - you'll also have access to our exclusive email list with even more free e-books and insider knowledge. Well, what are ye waiting for? Click the link below to join and set sail toward exciting adventures in American History.

Access your bonus here

https://ahoypublications.com/

Or, Scan the QR code!

www.ingramcontent.com/pod-product-compliance
Lightning Source LLC
Chambersburg PA
CBHW071457140726
47997CB00005B/1756